THE
NEW
VISIONARIES

Evolutionary Leadership
for a Vibrant World

by
Soleira Green

THE NEW VISIONARIES

Evolutionary Leadership
for a Vibrant World

by Soleira Green

Cover image:	© SuperStock, Inc.
Graphic Designer:	Dunstan Baker www.honeyrooms.com
Printed by:	CPI Antony Rowe 48-50 Birch Close Eastbourne, East Sussex BN23 6PE U.K. www.antonyrowe.co.uk
Published by:	The Evolutionary Network, 32 Millbank Burgess Hill, West Sussex RH15 8DD U.K. www.newvisionaries.net
ISBN #:	0-9529801-5-0

DEDICATION

This book is dedicated to all of you
amazing new visionaries out there
who are evolving our world.

SOLEIRA GREEN

Soleira is a global visionary, evolutionary leader, co-founder of The
Evolutionary Network and a passionate writer, speaker, trainer and
coach for all things new. 'The New Visionaries' is her second book
in print, written as an expression of her passionate commitment to
revolutionise the face of leadership on the planet today. Her first
book, 'The Alchemical Coach', sources the evolution of coaching,
empowering coaches everywhere to inspire amazing, evolutionary
contribution in all those they touch. Trainers for The Evolutionary
Network travel the world inspiring evolutionary living, leading,
coaching and vibrant being with individuals, groups and businesses
everywhere. To learn more about Soleira and her work, visit:

www.newvisionaries.net
www.visionaryleaders.biz
www.AlchemicalCoach.com

or contact her by email at soleira@newvisionaries.net.

THE NEW VISIONARIES

Evolutionary Leadership for a Vibrant World

by Soleira Green

CONTENTS

Chapter	Page #

Chapter	Page #

THE
NEW
VISIONARIES

Evolutionary Leadership
for a Vibrant World

by
Soleira Green

INTRODUCTION BY SOLEIRA

Welcome to the world of new visionaries ... people who invent
everything anew for the co-creation of a vibrant new world. This
book is an adventure into the leading edge of leadership today.
Throughout it we're going to traverse the realms of ......

- evolutionary leadership
- living vision
- transformative power
- vibrant energetics
- beyond self being
- collective consciousness
- true authority
- connective presence and
- the art of excellence.

No other leadership work I know covers the exciting terrain of
connective, transformative, evolutionary leadership. From here, the
world opens up its gateways to a vibrant, creative reality and we are
filled with the immense and wondrous power of potentiality. We
dive with great glee into visionary adventures that occur with the
ease, grace and playfulness that connective leadership offers.

As you enter the portals of its wonders and play, I wish you great
fun as you surf the possibilities and potentialities of your own
evolutionary contributions and the unleashing of the greatness that
is inherent within every single one of us. From this place, we evolve
from small people with complex, global problems to solve ... to
amazing beings contributing to the evolution of a magnificent world.
May you enjoy every moment of reading it, soaring with great glee
into every breakthrough you discover within these pages. A secret
hint to reading this is not to read it from an individual perspective
(i.e. rating or judging yourself on how you're doing with it), but
rather to read it as if every word you read, every feeling it
engenders in you and every possibility that arises from it are for the
conscious evolution of us all. Transformative, connective reading ...
why not!

A NEW PARADIGM OF LEADERSHIP EMERGES

A NEW ERA ... A NEW LEADERSHIP EMERGES

There's a new kind of leadership emerging in the world today. I call these new leaders **'THE NEW VISIONARIES.'** They're inventive, super creative and alive with infinite possibilities for how things can be. They're charismatic and definitely don't follow anyone's rules. They don't dwell on what is, nor do they try to change the old. They create, invent and evolve whatever they come in contact with in a leaderful new way.

These new visionaries are appearing in the midst of a huge evolutionary shift, a new era that is light years ahead of any cultural shifts we've seen in the last thousands of years. What makes this new era so amazing and different?

... Human beings are at long last stepping beyond being small people tossed around by the chaos of life to become vast and wondrous beings of pure possibility. We're learning to work with potential and to dance in the moment creating breathtaking new possibilities. A new visionary leadership is emerging that is brilliantly creative and inventive in limitless new ways.

... We're connecting all around the world, building a global community of inventive people who are passionate about Life, who want to see a better world for all and who are ready to live 24/7 to make that a reality now. The world is shrinking through new technology, arts and communication, resulting in the growth of people power. New visionary leaders are sourcing this shift to people power, connecting up their ideas, passions and visions with incredible speed, regardless of where they live, how old they are or how much money they have. They make the impossible possible with increasing ease and strength.

... We're moving beyond duality and polarity, at long last beginning to see that things are not black or white, right or wrong, true or untrue. We've gained a new freedom to see things from a wide

2

range of perspectives and this new seeing is liberating us from polarity into paradox and beyond. In paradox lies the rich understanding that all is not quite as it seems. That what is said, may not be what is heard. That what is believed as true today, might not seem quite so true tomorrow. That we just might be living in evolutionary times and nothing will hold to the scrutiny of an enduring philosophy. Isn't that just the most wonderful thing? The liberation of belief and of polarity and duality! Now there's a possibility that just might end wars on this planet for all time.

... We're discovering a new kind of leadership, one that inspires and empowers leaderfulness in others, that deeply and richly cares about the betterment of all, and that stands for a bigger, greater view of the world and beyond, to steward into play the evolutionary creations that are now ours to unfold. Visionary leadership ... living and leading beyond self ... a whole new playground of leadership and power. This is our journey throughout this book. The playful discovery of brand new ways to empower, enrich and enhance Life with every breath we take, every word we speak and every action we initiate. A brand new humanity. A stunning new world. Isn't that why we're here, to co-create a brilliant new future for us all?

THE NEW VISIONARIES

How would you recognise a new visionary leader? What differentiates them from other types of leaders?

- New visionaries don't protest what is. They celebrate what can be.

- They see what's missing and then identify the potential and work with it.

- They don't live in anyone else's ideas of what can be done. They invent brand new, exciting ways of getting things done, breaking the boundaries of known thinking.

- They live outside the rulebooks, choosing instead to create the reality of their dreams, rather than live inside someone else's version of reality.

- They empower leadership in everyone they work with, calling everyone into the dance of visionary creation. They know that they can't fulfil these huge visionary possibilities by themselves.

- They use communication, like television, mobiles and the internet, to connect them with the world of their visions.

- They know that what they're doing isn't about them. It's about the realisation of something more important than themselves. They live in and as the vision, thriving in the dynamics that visionary living affords.

New visionaries live beyond self. But don't get this mixed up with selflessness ... it's way past that. Selflessness and being in service are old concepts now. Visionary leadership is about vibrantly connecting to and working with limitless potential, always creating the next newest NEW. It's about soaring into new levels of being that allows us to co-create with great passion, vibrancy and vitality. It's a new kind of leaderfulness that celebrates the very best that every single person has to offer. It's a brand new paradigm of evolutionary leadership and power.

Want some well-known examples of new visionary leadership?

- Jamie Oliver and his 'school dinners' vision, supporting the well-being, growth and learning of our children in an increasingly non-nutritious world.

- Tim Smits and The Eden Project, paving out pathways of possibility for eco-environmental possibilities.

- Bob Geldof and Live8, bringing the global voice together to make poverty history by influencing decision making of the world's top leaders.

Throughout this book we'll be journeying into this new paradigm of leadership and power. You'll have the opportunity to take the steps yourself to becoming a new visionary leader as well as discovering how to empower it in others. But we'll also be getting to know some of the new visionaries throughout the world, demonstrating the unique ways in which they delightfully express their inventive leaderfulness.

Many of the new visionaries you'll get to know throughout this book are not well known ... yet! They're real people of incredible vision, full of passionate energy, creating the world of their dreams, engendering a richer, better world for us all. They're entrepreneurs, coaches, consultants, teachers, executives, futurists, artists ... in all walks of life and at all ages, they pervade our culture with new concepts and ideas that empower and evolve Life for us all. The new visionaries we'll be dancing with in this book are:

Alan Wilson ~ Champion of Children, UK ... www.alanwilson.info www.developyourchild.co.uk www.theenergyalliance.com

Annimac ~ Intuitive Futurist, Australia ... www.annimac.com.au

Dianne Kipp ~ Courageous Living Coach, USA

Ian Lewis ~ Founder of The Campaign for Adventure and Clerk to the All Party UK Parliamentary Group on Adventure and Risk in Society, UK ... www.campaignforadventure.org www.lifecollege.org

Jane MacAllister Dukes ~ Artist, mother of two magnificent new kids, trainer and co-founder of The Evolutionary Network, UK ... www.janemd.com www.evolutionarycourses.com

John Blakey ~ Group Director of Coaching for LogicaCMG and business visionary, UK

Marci Lebowitz ~ Co-founder of the Autism Center for Enlightenment, USA ... jewelmarci@aol.com

Mark Priede ~ Head of Coaching, ANZ Bank, Australia

The Mega Group ~ My wonderful mega buddies who've worked dedicatedly together over the past six years on the evolution of collective consciousness ...
Alice Finnamore in Canada (www.alicef.byregion.net),
Helen Rockliff in the UK (helen@evolutionaryliving.co.uk),
Pippa Lee in the UK (www.lifecollege.org),
Susan Friedman-Kramer in the USA (sfk9@cox.net) and
Trudy Zachman in the USA (www.zachmanmassage.com).

Neil Crofts ~ Founder of Authentic Business and author of 'Authentic' and 'Authentic Business', UK ... www.sevenstages.net www.authentictransformation.co.uk www.authenticeducation.org.uk

Sonia Stojanovic ~ Previously Head of Transformation, ANZ Bank, Australia; currently a management consultant in the USA, working globally for the transformation of business

Tim Laporte ~ An exec with a difference, previously general manager of a company in Australia ... tim@renovatio.com.au

And lastly, my wonderful husband, **Santari Green**, evolutionary magicaliser extraordinaire ... www.Imagi-Callity.com and me, **Soleira Green**, global visionary, author of 'The New Visionaries' www.newvisionaries.net and co-founder of The Evolutionary Network www.evolutionarycourses.com.

So, having made the initial introductions, here we go into an exciting journey for new leadership and power.

A NEW PARADIGM OF LEADERSHIP AND POWER

A paradigm is a way of viewing reality, a perspective that generates the energy from which culture gets invented and lived. Throughout the late twentieth century, we operated in an old paradigm of leadership and power, one that seemed to care little for the well being of people and of the planet. Resources (nature and people) were used up in the name of profit and power.

In the early 2000's we began to see an upswell of leadership associated more with social and environmental responsibility. A more caring and open approach was emerging alongside **a middle paradigm of leadership** that worked in service, with open door policies and a focus on people.

In the last few years (2004-2006), **a brand new paradigm** has arisen. We're seeing a completely new kind of charismatic, inventive, co-creative, visionary leaderfulness moving into play. It may not be fully visible yet in the halls of politics and big corporations, but it is emerging rapidly in individuals throughout all aspects of society and the world today. These are the new visionaries who are co-creating a brand new world.

Let's look at these three paradigms and see how leadership, power and vision are evolving within these new versions of reality:

PARADIGM	OLD	MIDDLE	NEW
LEADERSHIP	Dominating	Open & Willing	Empowering
	Hierarchical	Teams	Leaderful
	Competitive	Co-operative	Collaborative
	Overpowering	Serving	Inspiring
	Autocratic	Inclusive	Co-creative
POWER	Forceful	Soft	Vibrant
	Power over	Power with	Power of
	Individual	Others	Life / Potential
VISION	Linear	Progressive	Limitless
	Past-based	Responsible	Visionary
	Declining	Improving	Evolving

This new leadership and power is sourcing from a number of things:

1. An open, vibrant energy system that offers us enhanced abilities to see, sense and know beyond the traditional abilities that the mind alone can afford

2. A growing sense of inter-connection with our global identity, with the planet itself and with Life
3. A new level of being, which operates sourcefully beyond self.

Before we go on exploring the journey into new visionary'ism, let me introduce you to the first new visionary who personifies this new paradigm brilliantly in every way. I give you Tim Laporte, an exec with a difference.

NEW VISIONARY #1
TIM LAPORTE from Australia
Creating a whirlwind culture ...
An exec with a difference
tim@renovatio.com.au

I met Tim in Australia at our Evolutionary Coaching & Leadership course in May 2006. He had just left his position as general manager for a medium sized company to step into his next level of leadership. Throughout the course, I came to know Tim as a fabulous new visionary and was thrilled, as I listened later to his interview, to discover that he exemplifies all of the things that so many of us believe are required for the evolution of business today and that he has been able to produce extraordinary results (financial and otherwise) in the three companies that he's run so far.

During the interview, Tim talked about creating a whirlwind culture, meaning the name of the company (Whirlwind) that he worked for at the time. But after listening to the whole interview, I believe that Tim should coin the term 'whirlwind' culture as a new way of doing business, as that's essentially what he creates while he works ... a whirlwind of passion, excitement, exhilaration, movement, expression, abundance and success for the company and for everyone involved.

GETTING PEOPLE TO BE EXTRAORDINARY
"One of my first higher management positions was overseeing and running the housekeeping contract for the Olympic Games in Australia ... 24,000 beds and 6,000 bathrooms a day with 40 tons

of linen and 1,000 staff. I was left to run the whole show with complete freedom and I loved it. For the first time in the history of the Olympic Games, not a single bed was missed and profit came in 73% over projected figures.

One of my fond memories at the Olympics is standing up on a table in front of 400 staff at 6 am, speaking to them about the importance of being earnest of their morals and ethics. There had been some items that were stolen and I stood up and spoke to them about what stealing meant. How we had a very important task with the Olympics, and how we must have work ethics and work against any 'reproche' as we say in French. I don't know if it was my tone of voice or the words that I used, but I electrified the first group of people in addition to the next few groups. From that point onward, there was no more stealing. We're talking about people making beds and cleaning bathrooms that were focused on doing their jobs and excited about being involved in the Olympic Games. That's when I realised that I had something in me that could get people to be inspired about what they're doing ... inspired to think outside of themselves and to think of the bigger picture.

I have an ability to grasp the big picture and to voice that for others so that they can partner with the vision, align to it and express themselves passionately within it. My very first boss taught me when faced with a complex situation, I should look at it as if I was going up in a helicopter, removing myself from the picture, to see the bigger picture from a higher view.

I love working with others to get them to see the bigger picture and to generate vision and possibility for themselves. When visioning with a team, I very rarely put my own points forward and the outcome is really an amazing amount of energy. In one instance, we were working on some very big shifts within a company that was in acquisition mode and I remember being in the board room jumping up and down, getting completely energised and getting out of people what the solutions were and what we could do with them. I get people to think, talk and believe in their ideas and then I get them to dive back into it energised and inspired.

Then someone else says something and I drive that into its next level. There's so much energy created through this form of visioning and I get an amazing buzz out of it. I can get people on a high, thinking outside of their own boxes, where a whirlwind of empowerment and creativity gets created.

CREATING A WHIRLWIND CULTURE

After the Olympics, I joined a printing and design company called Whirlwind, as general manager for the New South Wales department. Once again I was fortunate to work for someone who just let me be. He said 'Tim, just make it happen' and I did.

In a year's time we went from $1 million to nearly $7 million and after a year they offered me the role of managing director of the whole group. I galvanised this business to the point where every one of the 105 staff was very proud to say there was a Whirlwind culture.

There was music blaring through loudspeakers in the general environment and anyone could walk up and change the music … and not once was there ever a problem around that. They could dress any way they wanted and the surrounding was very simple and very beautiful. Clients would come and sit in the office and go 'Wow, it's just so great here.' People were just radiating. We had very young staff, more or less out of uni, and they loved being there, being part of this business. They loved the energy that was present. And that showed itself in a massive growth in the business. When I left the business a year and a half later, it had reached $20 million in turnover and we'd made a massive profit. We were living the Whirlwind culture and we had people knocking on our door to work with us.

I had this guy come in for an interview feeling uninspired in his current position as general manager of another company. He said he was just checking it out. He didn't really need the job. I asked him back for a second interview and he said 'How can that be? I was really quite hopeless.' And I said 'No not at all. The words that you said weren't necessarily what I wanted to hear. But what I felt from you is that you're someone I want to pursue further for the role.' In the second interview he really relaxed, was more himself and I saw that he was the man for the job. He said to me very clearly 'I'm coming to this business because I want to work with you Tim.' I knew then that I must be doing something very different and that it was definitely working.

What was I doing that was working so well?

BEING FULLY MYSELF

I was being completely myself and empowering others to do the same. I believe it's very important to lead by example. I'd wear my good old Australian boots, jeans and a business shirt with the sleeves rolled up and no tie. That's my corporate attire! I actually negotiate that in my contracts. It's not my position that's important. It's how I am in it that makes a difference. You'd never see me sign an email 'Tim Laporte, General Manager.' I'd always sign things 'Ta, Tim.' The function doesn't give the power. Whether I'm in a suit or not is irrelevant! My role is not determined by what I wear, but by how I lead. It's who you are and how you interact with people that makes things happen.

By being yourself fully, you can do anything you want. Your dreams are boundless. By getting people to be passionate in love, life and themselves and to do what they love to do, it's a 360 degree opportunity. Then it's simply seeing where they are going from there. In life, you attract people on the same path who are very powerful and you agree to do some amazing things together. From a business perspective, if you help and let people be themselves, then you don't have to worry about the business anymore. The collective aspect of all these people goes far beyond people's expectations and you create something far greater and different. At Whirlwind, I remember clients looking around and going 'Wow, look what's going on in this place, all these people buzzing and laughing.' There's this incredible dynamic that kicks into play when people are being fully themselves.

I got to be fully myself by default. At the age of 20 I had two choices, one was to leave and another was to be here and alive. I actually made the conscious decision of living, to do something

11

with my life. I said I'm going to be Tim Laporte and stand on my own two feet. It was a conscious choice for me. Once I made the decision then I kept meeting really interesting people who kept showing me the paths to follow that led me today to being a 40 year old bloke leading a life that's just bloody marvellous.

But when people look up at me and go 'Tim, wow, you've done this and achieved that...', I think that's not what it's about. Cut the crap guys. It's about making conscious choices in our lives and not being afraid of moving forward. It's about having faith in ourselves. It's about people loving themselves, knowing that the world's their oyster and having life be full of joy, laughter and freedom.

FREEDOM, RESPECT AND THE BIGGER PICTURE

The key lesson for me in life was learning to love and believe in myself. To never forget to be passionate about life and love ... about everything. Once you do that, you just feel so good, you radiate as a human being. I give that to other people willingly, consciously. Freedom and respect comes through that. It's about accepting their differences. It's about listening to them powerfully. It's about accepting who they are and that's a very basic form of respect.

I let people have the freedom to do what they want to do and be themselves. I respect them and keep them informed of their part in the bigger picture. At Whirlwind, I'd have these brief stand-up meetings every Friday afternoon where I'd share with them the financials of the week, what we had achieved and where we were going. I remember having a bit of an argument with the stakeholders of the business where they wanted to withhold this information and I said 'Guys, the real power is not holding on to the information. The real power is sharing it.' I realised that my style of leadership is to share my vision, to share my understanding of business.

Showing them how they fit into the whole, it's nothing to take 15 minutes more to give the people who work for you the big picture. This let's them see how to make things happen as a whole for their clients and allows them to show their clients the bigger picture when they work with them. The people that work with me love this. If you treat people with respect and empower them with the freedom to do what they want to do, it always works out brilliantly.

LEADING, NOT MANAGING

I don't manage people. I lead them and that's a very big difference. It's about having highly energised people who work for themselves. Leading people is to share what I see. I have this ability to grasp complex concepts and to express them simply. I can talk about the same vision, but I can share it in different ways that works for the person or people I'm talking with.

I seem to be able to share this ability to see beyond one's self, to see what can be for them and for the bigger picture. I get people to dream, to give them hope and the desire to better themselves and to move forward. I get people excited to want to better themselves, to do things they haven't done before. I also give people some serious kicks up their bottoms if I feel they're not doing themselves justice. Mostly people have the potential if you just give them the opportunity to soar.

LIBERATING PEOPLE AND THE BUSINESS

At Whirlwind, if we had five objectives for staff, three would be professional and two would be personal. Through the business we would support them in their personal goals. So if that meant that they left the business, then we'd have a big party to celebrate that for them. If people stay with you for 2 or 3 years, great and if they leave after 6 months, that's great too.

One of my key managers was an artistic director that took me months to find. She fell in love with this guy from England and came to me after just a couple of months at work saying 'Can I take ten days to go to England?' I said 'Yes, go.' She came back to me after her trip and said 'Sorry Tim, I've got to go.' And I said 'Great.' You've got to be yourself and go when the next opportunity arises that's right for you. Because if it's right for you, it'll be right for the business too. The business will find someone else to do the job. It actually costs the business to keep people who don't want to be there anymore. The energy in a company takes off when you liberate people to be themselves.

MY VISION FORWARD

My vision forward now is to not be held back in any way. The last two companies I worked for, one way or another there was always a bit of hold back; they were stopped by their beliefs. So what I want for today and tomorrow is to work within a medium sized business with a couple of hundred people because that's a lot of energy and therefore positivity and opportunity in this size of company. The industry doesn't worry me at all. Whatever we have to deliver, I'll liberate people to make it better. I want to be in a position where there's no condition to my employment. I want a 'carte blanche' as they say in France, a free hand, and if the stakeholders of the company don't feel comfortable about that based on my past successes, then it wasn't meant to be. I want to do things differently, standing on my own two feet to make things work. I'll be accountable to a board or to people, report and all those things, but the running of the business and the decisions to keep it going need to be mine and be something that I can open up and share with the people who run the business. I want to offer my services to a company who's prepared to go to the next step, which needs and wants someone like me to lead the way for it. The role of leadership for me over the next couple of years will be in the form of someone else's business. And I'm very optimistic that I will meet the right people and that it will go brilliantly. I look to the future and my heart skips a beat ... I am standing on my own two feet looking into the horizon where the ocean breaks from the sky ... it's a beautiful life.

I'd like to meet some of the heads of large companies or industries to trial my ideas, thoughts and beliefs. I love a challenge. One of the challenges I'd love is to have a wonderful heart to heart with someone who's running a big business. When I finish my masters in business, I have this idea of writing a thesis on new leadership for a PhD, maybe something like the art of leaderful being. It's who you're being ... it's who you are that defines you and in there lies the art of real leadership."

14

OUR ENERGETIC EVOLUTION

So you've met Tim, our first new visionary. Isn't he wonderful? And you'll be glad to know that there are many more out there like him just waiting to be unleashed in terms of what they can achieve.

What is it that's shaping the face of new leadership today? What's so different now from the way it's always been?

OUR ENERGETIC EVOLUTION

In the past, human beings in western culture have been closed off from themselves, others and Life ... closed minds, closed hearts, disconnected from spirit and with souls tucked neatly inside away from the 'big bad world.' We've been living inside a closed energetic, one in which the world of energy and consciousness seemed to barely exist.

But today that's all changed. We have radically evolved our energetic blueprint over the past decade, moving us from a closed energy system to an open, vibrant one. The human heart has opened, the higher energy (spirit) has landed and the inner energy (soul) has flipped up from its safe space within to allow for a 'wholistic' integration. Discovering wholeness, we are moving beyond a 'mind only' approach to life into a powerful energetic connection with greater intelligence ... the living consciousness that surrounds and fills us.

We have entered an era of creation and evolution far beyond our wildest dreams. We are remaking this world and our place in the great cosmic swirl. We are stepping beyond 'seeking for answers in a chaotic universe' to living as sources for Life. It's not a religious step or even a spiritual step if you will. It's a becoming ... an evolutionary leap for the whole of humanity into a greater understanding of our role as conscious creators and evolutionary designers for a magnificent new future for us all.

It's in this free flowing, sourceful domain that new visionaries play. We aren't limited by any existing beliefs or faiths. Instead, we are

15

the creators of our own beliefs. We're making it all up in the moment, willing at any moment to surrender how we know things to be to discover the latest NEW. This act of surrender is so contrary to how things have always been on planet Earth that it's quite staggering to see the immensity of this simple willingness to let go and keep moving on with our understanding, wisdom and creations.

We're already seeing a mass 'opening up' throughout the planet. While many might not yet say they've opened their hearts and integrated their higher and deeper energy into a wholistic new level of being, they might say things like:

"I'm feeling a lot more free to really be me."
"I can't be untrue to myself anymore."
"I'm discovering a greater sense of purpose and meaning in my life."
"I want to make a difference on a bigger scale."

These statements, which are becoming more and more prevalent throughout the world today, are indicators of our energetic evolution. The human blueprint is evolving and we are living today in a brand new energetic (personally, globally and cosmically) that allows us to live as so much more of what we, as a race, are capable of being. We're reinventing human beingness and creating ourselves anew in an unlimited capacity.

FREE THINKING ... EVOLUTIONARY ABILITIES

In letting go of the old, closed ways and in opening up to a new sense of wholeness, we're discovering the ability to 'free think', moving beyond a mind only orientation to operate connected with the living intelligence that pulses around and within us all. It's like plugging the computer (the mind) into the internet (living intelligence) via a broadband stream (our new energetic connectivity). Liberated in our thinking and operating beyond mind, we discover that nothing is fixed and that anything can be explored and known. As we open up to the world of energy and to living intelligence, we discover enhanced levels of ability that assist us in a greater understanding of Life and our role in it.

These enhanced abilities, the tool kit for new visionaries, include:

Knowing

Knowing offers us a download of understanding and perspective that allows us to look beyond 'what is' to see what's really going on. Knowing can come from deep within as well as from the great 'out there.' It's not about ancient wisdoms. We're developing our ability to create fresh new wisdoms appropriate to each new moment. It's not about being a 'know it all.' It's about being connected to the knowing that is always there, just waiting for us to tune in to its higher frequency. It's not about intuition (gut feel), although that's a good first step on the journey. With intuition, you might not know why you're doing or sensing something, but with knowing you understand the whole thing from a variety of perspectives.

Innate sensing

Innate sensing allows us to energetically sense what's going on around us at various levels of vibrational reality. It's not about empathy (tuning in to the denser frequencies of emotion such as pain and suffering), although that's certainly one level of sensing. Innate sensing tunes in to the higher vibrational frequencies of potential ... the greater, deeper, more profound possibilities of what can be in any moment. Innate sensing can tell you a lot about 'what is', but with the full range of innate sensing, you're completely in charge of scanning the various levels of frequency to gain the information, insight and perspective that gives you the optimum understanding and movement that you seek.

Telepathy

Telepathy, by its simplest definition, is energetic communication. Communication occurs on many different levels, but generally we listen only with our ears and speak with our voices. But the true communication is actually happening on many other levels or bandwidths. Accessing energetic communication is like connecting via a broadband stream between you and the other person you're communicating with. You're in touch with the full, streaming, energetic content of all that's been sent and received on a wide bandwidth of vibrational levels. First there are the words the person is saying. Next, there's what he or she really wants to say, but can't find the words for or is holding back. Then there's what he or she isn't even consciously in touch with to know to say ... the as yet unspoken potential of the communication. Telepathy deals with the conscious and the superconscious ... the spoken and the unspoken. It's not about reading someone's mind. It's about listening with the whole of you to all that wants to be said on all the levels. As we reach into our energetic connectivity on these levels we discover a world of rich telepathic communication that takes us immediately beyond misunderstanding and misperceptions, into a world of completely hearing, recognising and honouring what a person is really trying to say from their deepest place. It takes us to the very source of communication to create breakthroughs in our ability to communicate with one another beyond the spoken word.

Hyper-speed thinking
Thinking is limited by a number of things, one of which is our belief in time. If you loosen this belief and know that time is a construct that we are completely in charge of, then you begin to 'free think' with greater speed. Can we only think at the same speed that we speak? Not so. Everyone I've ever met has had at least one experience of speed thinking four or five things in the space of a few seconds. In fact, this is more regular than we know. There's a lot more going on with our thinking minds than we allow ourselves to consciously connect to. We're processing so much information so fast that we've fabricated a belief that we'd be thrown into chaos if we let ourselves be in touch with the speed of it. But if you surrender to hyper-speed thinking, as many of our new kids are today, you discover that this is the free flowing connection that allows multi-channel capacity to pop into play in any instant.

These are just a few of the evolutionary tools of new visionaries. From the expansive, connective, vibrant reality in which new visionaries live, these are normal, every day abilities and the delight comes in creating the next leaps in evolutionary intelligence, abilities and communication from here.

With these new abilities intact, we're learning to be masterful with reality creation and we begin at last to know that **AS WE PERCEIVE IT, SO IT IS.** What we choose to believe and how we choose to see things completely shapes the reality we live in ... and not just on a personal level, but on every conceivable level. New visionaries dance with this, bringing their creations naturally and wondrously into realisation for all. They operate in the bigger energetic, in the fields of living consciousness and creation that are very present and available to us now.

The air itself has come alive with potential and creation. It's as if we stuck our hands through the fabric of reality and pulled 'free energy' from the other side through into this plane of existence. A brand new Life source pulses through our veins and fills us with vibrant energy and unlimited possibility. We're learning to play with potential, versus issues, with every breath that we take. Is everyone experiencing this? Perhaps not yet. But a growing number are experiencing this new level of energy and anyone who does seems to instantly become a new visionary as the energy of potential, creation and a new Life source pulses through them, urging them to express the creation of the NEW.

So let's meet our second new visionary, a perfect example of high frequency sensing and telepathic ability. I give you Marci Lebowitz from the USA.

NEW VISIONARY #2
MARCI LEBOWITZ from the USA
A Specialist in Working with Highly Aware People ... jewelmarci@aol.com

Marci Lebowitz is a wonderful example of an energetically aware new visionary who has taken on being a voice and catalyst for the recognition of limitless potential, especially within our new kids. Marci is a specialist in working with Autistic, Aspergers, Attention Deficit Disorder (ADD) and Attention Deficit Hyperspeed Disorder (ADHD) children and their families. As a new visionary, she's awakening us to the brilliance that can be offered to us by anyone if we just look beyond the traditional measures of contribution.

When Marci meets one of these special kids, she tunes in to their frequency and consciousness, which is very natural to her, and then telepaths to them that she knows who they are and is ready to be taught by them what they've come to gift her and the world. The results are amazing shifts in communication, behaviour, touch, connection and relationship ... and not just for Marci and the child, but for their families and teachers as well. As the child is fully recognised, honoured and allowed to gift their contribution, the field in which they operate is opened up and energised, affecting all within these kids' range. Within this, Marci herself is gifted with amazing new insights into the evolution of us as a species and how we can work in new ways to discover our fullest potential.

UNLEASHING THE GENIUS POTENTIAL

Here's a brilliant example that came in an email from Marci last summer in relationship to a child she was working with:

"Tonight, my favouritest kid (extremely verbal), says to me three-quarters of the way through our session, 'Marci, I'm supposed to teach you things, and guide you so you can do things.' I said, 'Yes you are, how do you know that?' He immediately responds, 'I don't know who told me, but somebody did. I just don't remember who it is. Are you ready?' Of course, I spent the whole session telepathically communicating to him that I recognized his genius, that I needed his help and guidance and that I was very open for him to teach me. It's really fascinating when they are verbal and repeat the stuff back to you verbatim. I also told him that I believed he was a genius and he looked me in the eyes and said, 'Of course I am, I know that.' When his dad asked him if he knew what a genius was he said, 'A really smart kid who knows all kinds of things that others don't know yet.' We must have hugged 30 times throughout the session and then at the end he asked if I would walk him and his father to the car and would I carry him on my back. It was the biggest love fest you've ever seen between me and a highly evolved 6 year old (with of course, a diagnosis of aspergers!). Hmmmmm. It's moving fast and fun!"

How did Marci get from being one of these kids herself to an evolutionary agent, a new visionary, for the limitless potential of all?

"If I look back to when I was a little girl, I see that I was always a new visionary, always seeing and experiencing things that other people were not, and holding those things to turn out in a special way. Of course it was very tricky for me at the time because I didn't understand my abilities or have anybody to help me cultivate them. One of my first memories of these kinds of things was at the Lincoln Memorial in Washington, DC at four or five years of age. There was an extremely handicapped and deformed child there and I found myself strategically moving to where I could see him and connect with him. I knew right then, at the age of four or five that I would be working with people like this and that it was important for me to develop this ability to connect with them.

CONNECTION AND CONNECTEDNESS

I have always had deep understanding about connection and connectedness and about people either being or not being in that. All my life I've tried to talk with other people about this, but until just recently couldn't get them to understand what I was talking about. A year ago I met Suzy Miller from Arizona who also works energetically in the higher frequencies and with the new kids. Meeting Suzy turned the light bulbs on for me and I was able to move into a new place of leadership with all of this. Prior to this, people were saying 'Marci there's something special and unique about you. You affect us profoundly.' But I didn't have the understanding of how I was doing it or how to talk about it with them. I felt like it ran me. So half the time with the energy and the dimensions that I experienced, it was just enough for me to keep myself upright because I didn't have anybody to talk to about it. But after meeting Suzy, another person who worked similarly to me, it just burst open and began to develop and be cultivated much more rapidly. I began to find language for what it was I was doing and people would go, 'Oh there it is.' And I would reply, 'Oh wow, yayyy.' So it's been a wild, evolutionary year for me.

LIVING A HIGHLY AWARE LIFE

Each week my vision gets clearer and more crystalline, refining more quickly all the time. I'm called to bring awareness to people about what it is to live a highly aware life. Most of the people I work with are highly aware to begin with. So they're already on this path in some form, exploring, trying to make sense of things and looking for some peace in their lives, whether they're the children I work with or adults. My vision is to bring this to more mainstream society by assisting highly aware people to access, understand and realise their potential, so they can open it up even more for the world as well as have more fulfilment around it in their own lives.

I took on being the voice for all of this in the world and discovered, by taking that step into my own leadership, that people, resources and opportunities began to flow easily to me, allowing for a more public expression of the vision. More and more it seems that people are ready to hear these kinds of visions now.

I work with children with Autism, ADD, ADHD and with parents who are dealing with these highly aware children, teaching them parenting skills, self-regulation skills, how to be connected to themselves and their kids and how to model this for them. I also work with a lot of adults who are highly aware, many of them tending to be chronically ill in great part due to their high vibrational, energetic sensitivity.

These adults and kids are offering us the opportunity to discover a whole different way of operating, a shift from old paradigm belief systems to new paradigm beliefs. As we move together into these shifts, I watch people grab onto their own visions and move powerfully into highly aware and connected lives.

THE AUTISM CENTER FOR ENLIGHTENMENT
I'm also one of the four founders of the Autism Center for Enlightenment (ACE). The foundation is bringing together all kinds of alternative services, programmes and support for families who are dealing with autism. It's the first model of its kind and it's going really well. All the paperwork is through and approved, so we're now an official entity and are focusing on fund raising efforts, which will start to pop in the next few months. Interesting of those of us on the board, the two lawyers have a son with autism who is amazingly gifted and aware. There's myself and my

own awareness and vision around that. And then there's the physician that I work with who treats children with autism. So there are four people holding a very high vision, each with very distinctly different skills. It's a beautiful collaboration.

But my vision doesn't stop just there. I'm also working with neuro-scientists on the creation of neuro-science research, which is figuring out how to study people like us. We need to be able to study and understand these unusual gifts and abilities so that they can be more available to the general public.

THE PLACE WHERE VISION LIVES

For myself, these abilities include a very deep connection to self and to God / Source / the deep Creator. It's about having that depth of a very intimate connection within one's self and also to have those same connections outside of ourselves. The way I work is to get in resonant frequency with where the other person is at that exact moment and really connect in with them deeply so that they start to become aware of what's possible for them beyond what they're living. It's not only about language and communication. It's an experience of being connected in a very huge, vast way. I've had people say to me that when they met me, they felt me inside of their soul and they'd never felt that before. It's because I'm helping them touch that place inside of them that's been lost, the place where vision lives.

For most people it starts around the low heart area because there are so many misconceptions that we have about ourselves, life and the conditions that have blocked us being able to live from that place of limitless potential. Then it's about expanding and moving deeper out of the heart, from the core of our being, into essence, into the deeper knowing. Sitting there, in the core of our being, lies the vision.

NEW LEADERS

I work with so many different people, like parents, who are dealing with a lot of issues. But when they get in touch with this place of vision, they move into leadership and can hold these bigger visions for the family, the community and for all of these kids everywhere.

Everyone I work with is a leader in the context or scope of their life visions ... some people in a smaller context, others impacting hundreds of thousands of people. It's all about leadership in a brand new way of being. It means not buying in to the old ways and when you're not buying in to the old ways, you're a leader.

NEW WAYS OF BEING

I'm doing this with the kids as well. These children represent to the world different ways of being. When I'm working with an autistic child and we're connecting and interacting, he's impacting me on profound levels and then I get to go out into the world utilising that information. That's a huge leadership position which then also allows him to be more comfortable in his own skin, aware of what his potential is, enacting that in the world.

Just by my being with people, they're opening up their potential to be leaders. We've had this definition of leader as 'one in every ten thousand and I'm out in front and it looks like this.' This is definitely old paradigm. The truth is you're a leader by your way of being and that revolutionises everything around you.

When I think about people that I really admire who've walked this Earth, I think about Gandhi who is one of my favourites. He represents a being state. It wasn't like he was trying to do or be anything grand. He was being and in that beingness people came in droves and he was able to communicate brilliantly with them. You can see that he was not participating in old ways of being ... and anybody can do that, even a six year old. They could say 'Hey this is who I am and this is how I'm doing things and that's it.' They don't have to engage in behaviours that everybody else is engaging in. And that's a major leadership shift that is coming into the forefront of the world right now as more and more people hold these kinds of visions in their consciousness and are being this new kind of leader.

As new leaders, we need to live inside the belief that anything is possible. We're about to access frequencies where we're going to see more miraculous things happen. We're going to see more leadership where people who've been doing their work for a long

24

time can come forward in an integrated state. Without force, simply by their way of being, they'll impact people on huge levels.

COMMUNION AND COLLABORATION

There's a paradigm shift occurring right now where we're discovering that we can be connected with others in a way where there isn't separation and there is communion and collaboration. It has to do with this new way of being that we're being called to, which equates to being connected to our selves, which equates to being connected to others, which equates to collaboration. It's about connecting with the deepest source, allowing me to be in collaboration with other people in ways that I've never experienced before. The ways I used to able to get things to happen by myself aren't working as well anymore, but it does seem to take off when I'm in collaboration with somebody else. Collaboration requires a fluid being state where there isn't this rigidity of myself, my defences and my issues. When I move to this new way of being, these things all clear very rapidly and connection and collaboration happens wonderfully. Being in that state all the time is what we're coming to, so when we're separate from it we feel it, are aware of it and can move right back to it again.

What it really takes to live in this new way of being, as a new leader and new visionary, is a willingness to live beyond what's comfortable for you. It's not about discomfort, but a willingness to explore. It's about knowing that there's more, being able to let go of and move beyond our conditioning and simply go with what we know is waiting for us. This can be the trickiest place for people, allowing themselves to go for the limitless potential of who they really are and live that in their every day lives. I find the easiest access to this for people is for them to experience it, feel it and sense it. Once they get a touch of the higher realm frequencies and the deeper, more connected place of vision, they find it virtually impossible to turn back to living a normal, disconnected life. They become highly aware individuals living connected, collaborative visionary lives."

OUR ENERGETIC EVOLUTION

EXPERIENCING THE EVOLUTIONARY LEAP

If you're not already experiencing this evolutionary leap in a conscious way, then let's play with these simple steps to open up to your / our evolutionary energetics:

1. Take several deep breaths and allow yourself to relax. Let go of the cares and worries of today, setting them to one side for the moment.

2. From the very centre of you, begin to expand the awareness of your energy out as far as you can. Are you as big as the room, the city, the world? Keep stretching that expansive awareness and if all else fails, simply imagine you're out in space looking at the Earth from the cosmic skies.

3. Notice how you feel as you get bigger and more expansive. Are you feeling liberated, clearer, lighter, perhaps more playful? Keep expanding from the centre point of you until you can get as big as the cosmoses and see how you feel. Here a powerful liberation occurs with a sense of physical, mental and emotional freedom that many long for.

4. Next see if there's an inner you that still hiding inside. You know, that vulnerable, beautiful, precious you that many people don't get to see. If you've got a you that's still 'in the closet' so to speak, then it's time to bring this you out into the light of day.

5. Take a deep breath and breathe the energy of that inner you into the space in front of you. All of you now ... don't go leaving some part inside in the dark still. It's time to play, time to discover the true and wondrous you and celebrate it for all the world to see.

6. Now that you're out, let the energy of this inner you play in the light of day, going wherever it wants to. Perhaps you'll

see yourself swimming in beautiful waters, skiing down a snow kissed slope, gardening on a beautiful summer's day. Whatever play the inner you wants to do, allow yourself the freedom to imagine it, to observe and witness it and to allow it to really come out and play.

How does that feel? Are you breathing easier? Are you feeling more yourself than before? This is where you discover the authentic true you as well as your ability to connect more powerfully with creation. Once this inner you is out AND the outer you is expanded, you'll discover the vibrant, energetic living space that new visionaries thrive in. New visionaries live in an expansive energetic reality, connected with a lot more of themselves and in touch with the higher vibrational frequencies of the new paradigm realities. It's here, in touch with the new energies of potential, possibility and Life source power, that we discover how to really bring potential alive. It's from here that we can truly connect with ourselves, others and the world in brand new, evolving ways.

OUR EVOLVING INTER-CONNECTEDNESS

In a closed energy system, we weren't connected to anything, not even to ourselves (inner being tucked away in the deep inner and higher being disconnected in the vast outer). In an open and vibrant energy system, we're discovering a growing sense of excitement and exhilaration about the world of possibility that's emerging from connective living.

Living connected to ourselves, others and Life, we discover a world of wonder that surrounds us. We FEEL our connection to nature much more richly than before. We SENSE a profound connectivity to people at their greatest levels of potential. We KNOW that we are ultra-connected with the Earth itself as a wondrous being and we begin to live beyond environmental responsibility, providing extreme care for Life in all forms, human, planetary and otherwise. From a connected state of being, this isn't something you have to train yourself to do. You automatically ARE it because you revel in the beauty of all that you connect with. You live in the dance of potential, beginning to see beyond 'what is' into the realms of 'what can be.' Next, you take the step from living connected into evolving connectivity and the ensuing tsunami of energy, passion, vision and creation carries you onto new shores each and every day.

Are you ready to try it out? If yes, then here are some simple exercises to empower connective living:

1. Think of anything you're passionate about and see what happens as you let that energy free flow through you. You may begin to tingle all over, especially in your hands. Your high heart (breastplate area) opens up and a fountain of vibrant energy pours on through you. This simple exercise opens up the inner core, giving room for the energy of passion, potential and Life power to flow on through.

2. Now connect with creation. Just intend it and see what happens. Allow the energy of creation to flow all through you. Don't try to contain this energy within your body or think about it with your mind. Let the energy free flow. Creation is too big to stay within a single body. It wants to explode into Life. You can do this simple exercise anytime you're looking for more ideas, energy and creativity.

3. Next, intend to connect with the new Life source energy, not just as it dances in the air around you, but also to the very source of new Life energy deep within. Most people experience this as a new connection to the deep eternal inner, which is completely available to us now. Once you've connected with this inner eternal Life source, then allow it to be a wellspring for new energy pouring through you now. Let it sparkle you up and rush through you from head to toe. Let it put a smile on your face and an exhilarated rush through your body. Then, once you've enjoyed it for a bit, allow the energy to fluidly move to source evolutionary breakthroughs for you and your visions.

How did you do with the exercises? How does it feel to be interconnected with vibrant energy, with creation and with Life source? Imagine if you could walk around like this every single day. Guess what? You can. New visionaries are doing exactly this. I won't say it's a 100% experience because we are in the midst of evolutionary shifts and that means lots of to'ing and fro'ing as we create and explore our new levels of being. But generally, this is a new state of connective being, a 24/7 way of living that we might drop out of occasionally rather than having to find our way into it every day. It's this simple movement into expansive, connective, sourceful living that is gifting us a brand new, beyond self, real-life state of being. It's offers us continual adventure into a world of our own imagining and creation. And with that, let me introduce you to our third new visionary who specialises in adventure and who's working on the vision ... well actually the reality ... of an adventuresome world!

NEW VISIONARY #3
IAN LEWIS from the UK
Founder of the Campaign for Adventure
www.campaignforadventure.org and
www.lifecollege.org

I first met Ian Lewis as a speaker at one of our Corporate Soul Conferences in 2000. It was here, in the space of new visionaries collectively at work on their craft, that Ian initiated the idea of the Campaign for Adventure, designed to create an adventuresome society with a healthy relationship to risk taking. Today, six years on, Ian is the co-ordinator for the Campaign for Adventure and Clerk to the All Parliamentary Group on Adventure and Risk in Society. Inevitably groundbreaking, these two groups have just had passed legislation supporting healthy risk-taking (receiving royal assent in July 2006). Also in July, following Ian's representations to both ministers and the cabinet, the Royal Society for Arts, of which Ian is a Fellow, was asked by Tony Blair, Prime Minister, to set up a Risk Commission to review the place of risk and enterprise in a truly healthy society.

Recently, in an article Ian wrote for the journal of the British Association of Nature Conservationists, he gave his view of being fully human, and perhaps this, more than anything, says what Ian is all about as a new visionary:

BEING FULLY HUMAN

"The significance of 'the spirit of adventure', as we meet with those who inspire us, is unquestionable. Who do we respect, who do we admire, who do we hold high? The spirit of adventure is always present with the visionaries, the determined, the tenacious, the motivators and the achievers. The spirit of adventure is so present in a realised human being it is very difficult to see how an education system for all, in a society which wants itself to evolve, can ignore or leave to chance, the origins of being fully human. ... As the Campaign for Adventure puts it: 'Life is best approached in a spirit of exploration, adventure and enterprise. Chance, unforeseen circumstances and uncertainty are inescapable features of life and absolute safety is unachievable.' ... Whatever happens between my writing this and your reading it lies in that glimmering, frightening, stimulating realm known as uncertainty. It is no bad place to live."

Ian is a fascinating man to know and a great friend to have on the evolutionary journey. He's an innovator extraordinaire, but in ways that most people wouldn't necessarily see. Like most new visionaries that I know, Ian IS evolutionary energy at work in the world. Here's what he has to say about the world of vision, leadership and energy:

"My work is adventure ... adventure in the arts, the spiritual adventure, the adventure in the aesthetic, entrepreneurial adventure, the adventure in just being yourself, health adventure and so on. Once you're free to live as yourself in these areas then you find yourself helping the future rather than hindering it: you become a part of the future and you know it.

My role as an adventurer is to help people see possibilities. As I move through people, they begin to see themselves able to change and willing to allow other possibilities for change. They can then

30

become a part of that change manifesting and then things can really move.

ENJOYING POSSIBILITIES

I see visions as possibilities that are already out there. It's a picture of what should be, needs to be or will be. A world without aggression, hunger and suffering is something that is there. All we need to do is to help people do things that are more helpful towards that vision.

The world has been stuck for too long in ancient paradigms. We need to be far more positive with far more concern for a new way. I don't think the new way would surprise too many people since so many people speak about it as some sort of utopia or with some sort of euphoria. But there are a lot of people who don't see this move to the new as their responsibility or their possibility. Underlying people's inability to see things in different ways or to see or grasp possibility is their inability to enjoy possibility. Enjoyment is absolutely central to the new. To be constantly inundated with possibilities can be very frightening for people. They spend their lives trying to create something solid and don't like to see that change.

The game for new visionaries is to open up different dimensions and possibilities for people so they can become the best dimensional energy they are and enjoy playing with it. We can enjoy all aspects of dimensionality, from physical energies (breadth, width, depth, air, water, land) to sensory energies (balance, stillness, sound, smells) to cosmic energies (being everywhere and yet being at one as well as experiencing our multi dimensionality). All these things are accessible by any individual provided they become confident of, and even amused by, playing adventuresome games with the physical and non-physical world. I help people enjoy playing with things. It's vital, as we work our way through the old paradigms to the new, to have a sense of personal sovereignty, a real ownership of self and self-responsibility and ownership of our own opportunities and possibilities in this dimension.

31

People shouldn't think because they come from a particular background or don't have so-called required credentials, that they can't achieve things. I come from a big family with a typical council house background and yet Prince Phillip has given me the use of Windsor Castle for three days and in November I'm running events in Buckingham Palace and in the House of Lords and House of Commons. I just don't see these things as amazing. I see these things as normal and that they'll be there … and then they're there. I'm contacted a lot by the media, but I don't have a picture of myself on stage pontificating. I do see myself as helping the media to become fully responsible and properly empowered to be able to write accurately what is actually out there. That's what I hold the space for in the future I'm working towards.

EXPECT THE FUTURE TO BE AS YOU SEE IT

I always expect the future to be as I see it and I'm really surprised when it's not that. It's about where I sense the world wants to be and where I'm at one with the world. Constraints are self-created and don't exist in my world. So for example, if I walk into a political meeting or go to work with youth groups, I can see that they're sitting in their view of reality. So I get them to walk through their imagination, to learn to live adventurously and to move into the future as it could possibly be. I hold the space for all the change to take place and evolve the size of that space to be big enough to allow all the changes to happen in the best possible way.

I can do this easily and naturally because I feel everything as pure energy. The place I exist is everywhere. I'm hardly me at all. Working as and with energy allows for a fluidity and malleability of movement because of the interconnectedness that's available in the energetic sense. The whole of possibility and the nature of current existence and what people call now are all one consciousness, the cosmos as a totally living consciousness of being. Once we can interconnect with and live as this, we can be the individual and the whole all at the same time and from this place, any given part of the whole can take total responsibility for as much as it wants to at any point of time.

THE DRAWING FORCE

The point at which someone decides they're going to take responsibility and live in a certain way is the point at which leadership kicks in. Leadership is a multi-dimensional energy. When someone feels or knows they're there for a particular purpose, the cause begins to bubble up and becomes present. The energy changes and becomes quite directional. Good leaders will have a very clear picture of where it's taking them. But with the greatest leaders, even though they have clarity along the way, there is something else ... a very powerful drawing force that gives them all the tools, skills and resources they need to get to where they're going.

Accessing the drawing force is about working to become more conscious of ever greater sources of energy and possibilities. I currently feel the drawing from two places. The strongest is into the cosmos, the dimensions that we would call space and time. The other is something that I feel strongly within ... my physical existence, my presence. It's about aligning the two and creating a bubbling lifestyle in the here and now that follows the flow of the drawing force.

THE EUPHORIC FIELD

When I feel for the future, it's a feeling of euphoria and fun. There are terrifically invigorating, enlightening feelings around when you're drawn to the right place. Ignoring the drawing force and not moving with it can be painful and deadening. Average is not good. It's where the very best and the very worst meet and that's not a satisfactory place. Drawing yourself to average is not enough. Always draw to the very best ... the right place for you to be, a place I call the Euphoric Field, an elongated Now, where 'Peak Experiences' (remember them?) abound and life energies play. In the Euphoric Field all is one and visions are realised.

There are people who want to stand out. There will be people who will be needed to show the way and not everybody will have to do that. It's a great euphoria in itself to be in the places you should be, to be the energy you should be. They're all great places to be as long as they're the right places.

New visionaries are the people who live in the right places for themselves. Some will stand out and some will not. But when you're near them, you'll know them. You can't avoid that energy, that presence. People who are not ready to change will be tempted to reject them and people who are drawn to change will be drawn towards them to share their energies happily.

This place is where everyone will eventually end up. It depends on how much you want to tie yourself down to the present. There is no such thing as not letting go in the new paradigm. It is all about letting go, feeling where you're drawn to and thoroughly enjoying being in that place. Underneath all this is the understanding that the cosmos will evolve as we evolve. It's a place to get to, an existence you can enjoy being in and adventuring through. It's about bringing the world back into the cosmos and into health and bringing that health energy into the possibility of the furthest and greatest future, which is now long overdue."

BEYOND SELF

THE MOVE TO WHOLENESS

For aeons, we've thought of ourselves as tiny beings, grains of sand in a vast and chaotic cosmos. Today, we're stepping beyond this view into an evolving sense of being ... living and leading for something magnificently brand new.

It's been a wonderful journey ......

The 1970's and 80's introduced us to a psychologically oriented view of life. Therapy, counselling, self-help and personal development all became popular throughout this time. We were working diligently on ourselves to clean and clear the way for the leap into the 21st century evolution of being.

From the late 1980's through to the early 2000's, many people began a journey of a different purpose. Moving away from the 3D world and its chaotic confusion, many of today's new visionaries left jobs, moved to the country, became entrepreneurs, travelled the world or went back to school, generally finding the spaces where we could open our hearts, dig deep into our inner selves and integrate our higher energies on the pathway to creating wholeness for ourselves. We were creating and beginning to live the new blueprint for an evolving humanity and vibrant reality.

In the early 1990's, wholeness was a concept that you might be able to achieve some day if you really worked hard and focused your life upon that goal. But today, if you ask a room full of people how many of them are experiencing wholeness now, you'll get anywhere from 20% to 100% depending on the level of the audience. Isn't that amazing! In the 1980's if you had asked an audience if they felt whole, I doubt that anyone would have even considered putting up their hand. Having reached an integrated sense of whole self as a living reality, we could finally take the next evolutionary leap beyond self.

2005 was about that step ... a brand new way to be, an emerging new being'ness that offers us richness, fullness, aliveness and more. The whole of that year was about letting go and becoming something new and more. Many people around the world experienced this and became it without necessarily understanding the full scope of what they were a part of.

This is an evolution of being that we are co-creating and birthing. As conscious creators, we are remaking ourselves anew, liberating ourselves from the past and how we've always been and creating a marvellous new connectedness with Life and ALL. In this simple yet profound step, all of Life comes alive and being'ness evolves.

Remember, this is a paradigm shift and it won't serve us to look into the old paradigm of 3D reality to see if this new possibility of being is here and available now. Of course there are wars and manipulation and all that goes with old paradigm leadership and power. But the old is rapidly declining in energy and substance and the less energy and concern we give them, the sooner they'll cease to exist in consciousness as well as reality. What we give energy to increases, so new visionaries give their energy, passions, inventions and visions to the creation of the NEW and it's here that the new paradigm reality abounds.

Corporations today are a'buzz with the increasing need to establish social and environmental responsibility programmes and to pull the best out of their people. People power is forcing this level of responsibility upon them whether they want it or not. Look at the G8 leaders using words like collaboration, stewardship and an agenda for a better world at their 2005 summit. The 3D, old paradigm world is beginning to recognise the increasing need to align with this shift and is making its way towards a new paradigm of leadership and power.

If you look with fresh, new paradigm eyes, you'll see that today human beings are stepping, at long last, into a wholistic level of being ... and from here, from wholeness, we discover new possibilities for our future that lead us into living and visioning beyond self.

NEW VISIONARY #4
SONIA STOJANOVIC from USA
Love, Meaning and the Whole Person in Business ... Organisational Transformation

As the Head of 'Breakout' and Cultural Transformation for Australia's ANZ Bank, Sonia has created breakthroughs for organisational transformation over the past decade. Today she is working with a global management consulting firm in New York, about to move to the South African office of the firm. Her aim is to work within the mainstream of management consulting to bring this transformation to client companies while also influencing the social fabric of a country such as South Africa, during its post apartheid era. She brings passion, invention, connection, intellect and wholeness together into a wonderful demonstration that any and all of us can influence Life on what she calls 'this blue planet marvel.'

LOVE, MEANING AND THE WHOLE PERSON IN BUSINESS

"My vision is to bring love into business. To recognise that everything is love, that business doesn't need to be the kind of 'dog eat dog', hard-edged, market driven process, which we see developed in its biggest extremes today. That it can return to shareholders while also contributing to the community, giving meaning to peoples' lives and making a larger contribution. Business has been given a licence to operate by its communities and also by this very planet ... and this licence brings with it responsibility ... waking leaders and organisations up to this bigger role is what I am about.

My work seeks to address not only the big picture, but how it is translated at the level of the individual and their contribution. This is about getting people and organisations to have the courage and energy to look at and accept that the whole person has a place in the workplace, as opposed to the historical perspective that subscribes to the adage that the person who turns up for work is part of a machine as a human resource. It's about having the recognition that the whole person has a whole life and that we don't have to turn off parts of our lives and ourselves as we walk in the door. Once we can get people to get that, then they're up for doing the transformational work. This shift in root perspective is key to the work that I do.

They can then support their teams and businesses to go through processes that assist people to make the necessary choices that recognise that there is choice to reintegrate the mind, body and spirit ... that all three do matter to all of us. The key is to have people get, while taking them on a personal journey of transformation, that we are also able to measure and track that it's good for business. It does have to have a positive impact on business performance and not just be a touchy, feely, nice thing to do. We can prove this impact now on a wide range of measures. It makes intuitive sense that if people are their whole selves and are authentic with each other that the positive relationships that result will produce an up lift in productivity. We can offer that as the strange attractor to others to follow suit.

THE STRANGE ATTRACTOR

You know that restaurant scene in 'When Harry Met Sally', where the woman says 'I want some of what she's having.' When someone sees that someone else is having something good that they don't have, it's becomes the strange attractor. This is one of the ways to influence global culture shifts. We demonstrate that it can and does work and then others begin to want some of that. Once in the door, we work with people and organisations in a transformational way and the productivity, creativity and engagement becomes a fait accompli.

In my travels around the world, working for organisational transformation, I'm now seeing a big shift towards more people focused business. I believe this is due in great part to three things:

1. There's got to be a better way

The baby boom generation are the ones now leading these big companies and the baby boomers were either involved in, or on the fringes of, the 60's when the idea of love, peace and all that stuff came in to the vernacular. They've gone through their 'making hay while the sun shines' days and they're in their mid 50's and 60's now reflecting back, as I do, on what that was all about, thinking 'there's got to be a better way.' Also as we begin to see our own mortality with our parents passing, the questions arise in our minds ... 'What is my legacy? What am I leaving for future generations and how will I be remembered? Do I need to be concerned about the future I am leaving behind for future generations in a wider context?'

2. Young people on the leading edge of change

The younger generations, particularly GenY, are saying very clearly 'We don't want to be like you. In fact in some ways we resent the way you are, the 'me only' generation, only focussed on your own immediate satisfaction and we want something different. Yes we'll come and work for you and of course your money is important, but that just gets us in the door. So unless there's the challenge and the contribution that we want to work for, then we're not going to stay.' This is a generalisation, but it does seem that young people are the ones on the leading edge of change. They rattle things from inside, demanding that things be different. I feel this pertibation of the field of business is a healthy one.

3. Hundreds of thousands of us

There are hundreds of thousands of us out there, if not millions, working on these big visions. I run across them every day in my travels around the world. They may be people who are doing similar work to my own, in business, the community, schools, government, or they're people who are packing groceries in the supermarket that you strike up a conversation with or a taxi driver who tells you his life story on the way between home and work. There's a lot of thinking and reflecting going on out there. If you allow yourself the time to check into it, you find it everywhere!

What I've been finding is that if I shift the way I be to connect from a deeper and less superficial level, then people are more likely to have far deeper and more meaningful conversations ... conversations that are transforming the world, one at a time. It's those conversations that you can have at any moment of the day that truly are a blessing. What I find so interesting is that I'm often more 'out there' when I have those kinds of conversations one on one with people than I am in a corporate setting. I can try things out that I would be more circumspect about within a corporate setting. It's very fascinating to find how people respond when you talk heart to heart with them. Yet organisations are made up of people just like this, people with hearts, but something happens when we walk in the door with our hearts closed.

A GLOBAL NEURAL NETWORK

Being a visionary gives me the opportunity to really play at the edge and I love that. That's part of my contribution, as is connecting people. I'm always looking for opportunities to put people together with each other. I have this vision of having a neural network of people covering the whole globe. The reason that I'm happy and love going to different parts of the world is because it gives me the opportunity to taste that part of the world and where it's at, to see what's ready to be birthed and to meet those who are on the journey, to discover who's available for the work. At the moment, I'm focussing a lot of my energy on South Africa, but have also been working in Canada, the Middle East, Brazil and the USA. I'm going with the energy of working globally wherever there's an opening to engage in this new way and to co-create this neural network of like-minded people who share the vision.

ORGANISATIONAL TRANSFORMATION

My time and experience at ANZ Bank has led the way for me to be a spokesperson and catalyst for organisational transformation. I was offered the opportunity to operationalise the transformation of ANZ as a business as the Head of Transformation reporting directly to the CEO, working very closely with him around creating a breakout in the cultural transformation of what was a pretty broken culture.

'Breakout' is action focused towards breaking away from the past, being a different organisation and bringing hearts AND minds to work. What I learned at ANZ, apart from the power of working with energy, is that we can create transformation as a way of being, a way of life, a continual process that is consciously chosen within an organisation to become more of what it's meant to be and for people to become more of their own potential. That's what happened and continues to happen under my successor Siobhan McHale at ANZ. We were able to integrate it as a way of being into the organisation. There were a number of contributing factors that helped us to achieve that, as opposed to one thing that created the paradigm shift:

- **We created a whole system buy in.** With organisational transformation, it's got to be more than the traditional meaning of having the CEO and the leadership team on side as platitudes. It's absolutely critical that the whole team is on board for this kind of change. Consequences for non-alignment are key as role modelling, formal and informal, is a key aspect from the leadership. Some of our competitors tried to go down the same path without this kind of commitment and alignment and it didn't work for them.

- **We had to learn to let go of the past and live in the present.** We needed to put in place structures and safe processes for people to forgive and sometimes to confront, to let go of their withholds and to move on into the present. So many people in organisations are actually living in the past whilst trying to act effectively in the present through strategic intent. But they're not really in the present, not in the now, and hence are not as effective as they could be.

- **We used story telling with metaphors and real life stories about real people from all levels of the organisation,** who they were, why they believed they were making a difference and why their contribution was important.

- **We learned to break old rituals in order to allow new ones to be birthed.** So things like celebrations and little things like thank you's, things that normally weren't common within the organisation became important. We saw that it was important to 'take the time to smell the roses' so to speak.

- **We celebrated people who discovered that they wanted to do something else besides banking.** Instead of chastising them, we made that cause for celebration, a part of finding themselves. We made that on a spiritual level a part of the contribution, which would then enable others to be attracted to us as the next part of their journey. In practical terms that shifted us from being the least preferred employer in financial services in Australia to being the most preferred over a period of about two and a half years.

- **We began to attract people who were very much of the heart profile,** people who wanted to be involved in something where they could make a difference. Heartfulness and business focussed is a very powerful combination that is inspiring to self and others.

- **We introduced a compelling aspiration that gave meaning and purpose to the organisation.** The aspiration was not something that was dictated from above, but emerged from the energy of the field of banking in Australia. We talked about the 'Bank with the Human Face' and that worked very well for our people given that in Australia bank bashing is considered a national sport and very deeply ingrained into the psyche of the Australian people. So moving our people from saying they were ashamed of working for a bank, which we discovered in our initial rounds of diagnostics, to having people say they were proud of what we were doing was a big accomplishment.

- **We created the employees as part of the legacy,** recognising that they were part of that journey, being able to tell their kids and grandkids one day, 'I was there when ANZ decided to change the world of business and banking for the better.' They understood that the bank's vision and their part in it could contribute to their sense of having accomplished something in their lives. Allowing people the space to ask the question as to why they came to work and what was meaningful for them was a key consideration.

- **We worked on people's personal transformation from the inside out,** allowing them to transform their relationship to who they were, which meant business and the bank was transformed along with them. We spoke of the ripple effect and how it all starts with each of us being accountable for creating the future.

- **But we also worked from the outside in by transforming the organisational environment through policies, systems and procedures.** That was the non-sexy part I suppose. We changed the performance management systems, introduced a diversity agenda, a free internal job market, a bureaucracy alert to do away with bureaucracy and transparency around remuneration. We launched new recruitment processes, introduced a balanced scorecard, strategic reviews and all sorts of things that looked at creativity, growth and how to create innovation. Then of course there were things like the community agenda with volunteering leave (one day's paid leave per year to do community work that a lot of people did in teams), the first ever national literacy survey, financial literacy training run for the community out of the bank branches and match saving schemes for underprivileged people to go towards their children's education.

It was amazing to be a part of all of this and I guess being in the middle of it all, it seemed there was always more to do, more challenge to continually raise the bar. But one morning in 2003 I woke up and knew that I'd done what I'd come to do. I knew that it was time for me to move on. I didn't actually leave until July 2004, but during that time I worked with my team and the CEO to put the transition in place for my replacement, Siobhan, to take over. As part of the transition, there was a strategic review around 'Breakout' to determine the future focus for the work.

Prior to my leaving, we had started doing work on establishing an internal coaching programme for excellence with the dream that everyone at ANZ would be a coach for everyone else ... 360 degree and in the moment.

This came to me as a waking dream ... one of the ANZ values was to 'lead and inspire each other' and I had awoken that morning realising that through becoming a coaching organisation, this value would be realised. Once that was started, I knew I could leave and within a short period of time I found myself invited to New York to do the organisational consulting work that I now do globally.

GOING WHERE NO MAN HAS GONE BEFORE

For me, being a new visionary is about following the dream and following your heart, believing and knowing that the universe supports you and your visions. New visionaries are people who can go into the void and access what is waiting to be manifested into reality, translating that so that people can actually hear it and work with it. My sense of the power of the new visionaries that I'm seeing these days is that they're not sitting on the top of their hills with their mantras being righteous. They're very practical and out there getting their hands dirty. They're actively doing the work. New visionaries are up for it and as they say in Australia 'they put their balls on the line.' They're courageous and willing to go where no man has gone before, ala Captain Kirk, and then see how it grows. They're not fearful about making it up as they go along, to see what fits. I think that's the most exciting thing about the new visionaries that I'm seeing these days. They're up for it and are very substantive physical entities as well as emotional, mental and spiritual entities. It's about the integration of the whole. They are standing in all of those worlds powerfully and that's what the planet needs.

THIS WONDERFUL BLUE MARVEL

People with a spiritual calling often have a great desire to escape to the other dimensions, whereas I have a very different attitude around that. My sense is that when my time comes to leave this dimensional wheel of incarnation, it will happen at the right time as everything does. But there's much beauty in this world. This is an amazing place where you can eat wonderful food, drink great wine, laugh at jokes, cry at sad movies, look at the beautiful tree outside your window and marvel at all the very special creatures on this planet. I believe this is a very special time to be alive, to be

44

a loving and nurturing supporter of Mother Earth in all of her glory and my sense is that the new visionaries are in that space. They're very much about the practical ... how we can ensure the thriving survival of this wonderful blue marvel in its earthly reality and its consciousness.

This is the most exciting time of my life. I've been very blessed and my life experience has given me an understanding of the reason I'm here. I'm a new visionary and I get to bring my visions alive in the world at a very special time. But I'm also really grateful for the opportunity to link around the world with others of like mind and vision, of which there are many. People today are willing to go more deeply and are up for seeing the potentiality and for working in consciousness. We are in a time of exponential growth, a time when more and more people are finding themselves in transformational movement, discovering new levels of themselves and their potential to contribute to this amazing world in a multitude of ways."

BEYOND SELF (Contd.)

BEYOND SELF ... A NEW BEING EMERGES

Over the past decade we've been integrating our wholeness, learning to live in healthier ways in relationship to ourselves, others and the world around us. It's from here, this new sense of being whole, that we begin the journey beyond self where we rediscover a vast playground of extraordinary wonder, where we tap the limitless energy of creation and the unbounded presence of sourceful vibrancy.

The step beyond self is more than just a re-orientation from small beings trapped in individual and separate experiences. It's a complete revamp of being, a delicious, delightful co-creation of what's possible for being alive ... working, living and playing for the enrichment of Life.

Beyond self is not about selflessness. Far from it. The more you're willing to let go of the self you've always known, the more you discover a you you can't even imagine. In other words, the less you focus on the you you THINK you are (from your genetics, history, lineage, learning and past experience), the more opportunity you have to become all that you, and therefore we, can be.

This beyond self step is more than just an evolutionary move by some individuals to experience a more enlightened state. It would be a mistake to think that's all this is. Beyond self being is a brand new level of being for human beings. It's a complete redesign that inspires us from the inside out, upside down and all the way through. It's a step into the evolution of our collective nature and the possibilities and potential that we carry.

We're taking this step as a world, all together in one gigantic leap, whether we're all conscious of it or not. I see it all around me and in all the people I meet, whether they've worked with me before or not. So let me introduce you to another amazing new visionary who personifies this leap, a superb dad who was inspired by his daughter to take on creating the space for our kids to grow up brilliantly in.

46

NEW VISIONARY #5
ALAN WILSON from the UK
Champion of Children
www.developyourchild.co.uk
www.theenergyalliance.com
www.alanwilson.info

I met Alan Wilson two years ago at the first 'Children of the New World Conference' in the UK. We were drawn inexplicably together across a crowded room, both of us having identified a wonderful potential that was filling the room. Today, two years on, we're great buddies, having travelled together in the UK, USA and Australia to make our visions a reality.

Ten years ago, Alan tells me he was a stressed out, materialistic business owner, driven by money and success, with little time left for his family and kids. Two years ago, he was a renewed dad and a man with a vision to wholistically develop millions of children globally. Today, he's full of passion and possibility, a living example of the move from a man with a vision to a visionary who's working multi-faceted in brilliant new ways. In the past two years, he's:

- written and published a book entitled 'Listen to Your Children'
- has a second collaborative book underway with experts from all around the world on the evolutionary world of kids (to be published fall 2006)
- developed four programmes for teachers and youth workers to deliver and seven specialist programmes for coaches to deliver to parents, carers, teachers, foster carers and other professionals working with children
- initiated a charity, the Develop Your Child Foundation,
- founded and runs 'The Energy Alliance', a global affiliation of people who are working energetically in leading edge ways with new kids
- taught courses in communication skills for families as well as empowerment courses for a wide range of parents including teenage mothers and foster carers
- begun designing a vision for a new kind of school that supports the new educational desires and passions of our new

kids based on exploring their innate abilities and engaging parents in the process
- been working in a school with teenagers and their parents, teachers and staff to create an ethos of respect and empowerment and
- organised an international conference called 'Kids Are Really Different These Days', bringing together four leading edge pioneers from around the world to offer a breakthrough look at the evolutionary world of children.

Alan is a new visionary who knows how to get things moving and who puts his passion for kids at the very top of his life priorities. I give you Alan Wilson, new visionary and champion of children.

"I didn't know when I became bankrupt in 1993, with a life dominated by material possessions and a drive for success, that I would end up where I am today. Thank goodness for bankruptcies and the like ... events that force us to awaken from a very deep slumber.

All of a sudden the life I had was gone and the biggest challenge of that was facing myself as a failure. I was totally driven by ego back then and the ignominity of the failure drove me deeper into despair. Amazingly, this pushed me over the edge into a breakdown of sorts, but which I now call my biggest wake up call. It was then that I started to ask myself what life was all about. At the time, I know I was frightened about what the answers might be, but I look back now with a big grin and see how brilliant it's all turned out to be.

A SECOND CHANCE

It's given me a second chance at life ... and not just with my own kids as a dad, but as a person being able to realise my own potential and to help others, especially children, to realise theirs. Like any dad, when your children are born, you're awed by these little beings that come in to your life. With all of my three kids, I was fully participative in feeding, changing, getting up in the middle of the night where I could and looking after these wonderful little beings. I've always loved my kids, as any parent would say.

But during my married years, I didn't really take a lot of notice of the kids. I didn't engage with them as much because I was busy building the business and unfortunately at the time I didn't make them a high enough priority. I was always a good parent within my criteria ... that's to say, after my divorce, when I only had my kids for one day a week or a weekend every other week, I did learn to apply myself purely to them. That's what's really changed I suppose. When I was first married, they weren't a high priority. When I was divorced they were a high priority when I had them. And now my life is dedicated to changing children's lives forever.

Cassie, my third child from a second marriage, was a very big influence on this. I often refer to her as the reason that I'm doing this. When I think about it now I realise that I was so pleased to have a second chance to make up for the mistakes I'd made in my first family. My second marriage didn't last, but when I walked away from the marriage, I felt really bitter with myself that I couldn't make up for my earlier mistakes with Cassie. The breakthrough in our relationship as daughter and dad came when I took her on holiday for the first time to Majorca when she was 3 or 4. I started a diary called Cassie's Magic Moments, making this fabulous record of all the things she said and did on that holiday. I realised then that we had a very special relationship and that she wanted me as a dad. It was ok. I'd been given my second chance.

From then on everything became different. I started to repair myself and make it better with Cassie and me. Our relationship has blossomed and grown and maybe that's what's touched and sparked the visionary in me.

UNCONDITIONAL LOVE
It was like a big veil lifted off me. I had so desperately wanted to be a dad for her and despite all the circumstances with the divorce and the lack of opportunity to make up for my past failures, all of that was overcome by this little person's preparedness to give me another chance. It was seeing her in her magnificence and realising that this little person knew so much, that I knew I wanted to give every child that opportunity to have that feeling, the feeling of being unconditionally loved. Kids give it to us, but

49

we don't always give it back to them and that's partly I think because blokes especially don't find that easy to do. And certainly for me, I didn't realise I hadn't loved myself all my life, until that point when someone was unconditionally loving me.

This unconditional love unleashed something in me. It was the desire to make things right for kids. And so I began, not knowing exactly where it would lead me. It certainly wasn't the traditional, successful route I'd had planned for my life. But all I can say today is thank goodness it's gone this way.

By 2002 I had the passion to wholistically develop millions of children (as whole beings) globally. Then last year, 2005, I wanted to create better family relationships with my focus more on parenting. And now today it's to create the right community environments for young people to blossom and grow into the wonderful creative individuals they are.

CONNECTING WITH A POWER BEYOND ME

I'm not sure at what point I actually grew into being a visionary. It wasn't necessarily the moment I chose to do something for children. It's more likely when I started looking further a field from just the kids themselves, when I began to look into all the other influences (parents, teachers, peers, schools, education, etc.) that I became a visionary. I began to actively affect all those influencers to respect, listen and value these young people. I began to tap into a bigger picture and put my focus on supporting other people more. Not only does this take away our own issues and challenges, but it actually makes the whole thing ever so easy to do. It was here, operating beyond my own normal concerns for self, that I became more connected to and a part of the bigger picture and began to experience my own effect or influence on a power beyond me.

I'm still experiencing even now what this actually means and still asking myself questions about my responsibility to the world, to a bigger picture and to the collective. Again it's unconditional love for more than me, for a power beyond me that I'm connected to.

When I recognise that I'm connected to this power, then everything around me just changes and flows for what is a bigger purpose, which I'm part of, responsible to and finding my way towards. The more I do when I'm connected to this bigger power, the more creative and effective I become and everything is easy around me. This can be extraordinarily exciting and even a little uncomfortable at this stage of my growth.

So what is this power beyond me? I might call it the collective consciousness of all. It's where people of like minds or faith or trust are connected to take forward what wants to happen in the cosmos. We're all connected to that in some way or other. I guess the work I've done on myself over the last few years has enabled me to connect on a wider bandwidth, allowing me to tap into all there is, to contribute my part of life's rich tapestry.

From this place, not only do you connect and empower other people, it's an incredible way of life and attracts equally awesome people. I can see that in the past, I've limited people by holding them in a smaller space and that hasn't served me, or them, well. But connected to this power beyond self, it seems you naturally attract wonderful people who are awesome in their own unique ways and they dive in to help and to contribute what they have to contribute with our shared visions.

BEING A VISIONARY IS MY LIFE

Today I know my children are well looked after with fabulous mums and so I can focus a level of determination and commitment to the work that I'm about. It's what I can provide and what I want to provide to move the work onwards and forwards ... the work being the fulfilment of that bigger picture of what we're all here to do. So today being a visionary is my life, in every aspect. It's not just something you do. It's not a job. It's a life purpose. It's who I'm now coming to be. I think being a visionary is an ongoing evolutionary process that seems to have endless, incredible, breakthrough movements associated with it.

I seem to have had so many incredible ah ha's and life changing moments as well as profound experiences that have shaped my

51

growth and the development of my work. It has all been from real life experiences, not from a research or book study point of view. It's more about getting out there, knowing what's working and what isn't and doing something about it. And that's actually what I've done. When I've found a gap, I've done something about it … and there seems to be an increasing number of gaps and creations to fulfil them. Maybe that's the step from having a vision, like a project that you work on sometimes, to living 24/7 as a visionary. If I have an idea and I believe it's right, I'll go out and do it. I make things happen along with amazing, valuable, incredible support from some fantastic and awesome individuals. I love that about being a new visionary. There are so many others to play with to make it all happen with great fun and ease.

I've always had a good sense of humour and been able to laugh easily (mostly to myself or at myself). But life is so fantastically enjoyable as a new visionary that it takes joyful living to a whole new level. When you realise that you are creating your own reality, there's no one else to hide from. You stop putting your attention on yourself and start putting your attention on what really matters to you, to others and the world.

SIGNING ON FOR THE BIGGER GAME
I would recommend that others sign on for the bigger game and become a new visionary. They would need to suspend belief about themselves, understand the reality that they create around themselves and be able to unconditionally love themselves to connect with and empower others.

Two years ago I had a passion to wholistically develop children globally. Today my vision is to create community environments where young people can blossom and grow into the wonderful creative individuals that they are and where families can live whole and fulfilled. When I look back on that initial vision now, whilst it was a passion, it appears empty by comparison to the energy of what I'm about today and it's almost frightening what is going to happen in the next two years. But I am up for it. I'm really excited about the potential and impact on young people and families everywhere."

BEYOND SELF (Contd.)

THE BEYOND SELF YOU

I'm inviting you to take the step beyond self throughout this book and with that, to discover a life of unprecedented ease, of magical wonder and alchemical delight. Sound too good to be true? Believe me, it's completely and totally available for everyone now, with grace, simplicity and ease. If you're ready, read on and open the door to the life you've always wanted ... for you, for those you love, for the world and beyond!

Are you ready to adventure into new territory to discover an amazing new YOU? Let's go then. We're going to take the leap right to it ......

1. Set aside all the thoughts and beliefs about who you are. Be open to a brand new you.

2. Open yourself up to the vast, higher, external YOU and to the vast, inner, eternal YOU. This isn't just about opening your heart. It's about opening to ALL there is ... everything in all the cosmoses everywhere. Go on, you can do it! Throw back your arms and open up your chest. Reach out to the whole of you. You've always known you were much more than who others have seen you to be. You knew it from the day you were born. You knew deep inside of you that you were different somehow, here for a greater purpose even if you didn't quite know what that was. Well now it's time to own that, to become it and to live as and for it. This isn't about ego. That's an old paradigm concept to keep people small and in check. Own the huge, vast, amazing sense of YOU that's always been there, even if set to one side or covered over with the illusion of normal life. We all have this sense of a greater, deeper self somewhere inside of us. This is who we truly are and who we came here to be. So one, two, whoosh, let yourself be it. You're magically all that you are and can be. Just be willing to experience it energetically and let the energy do the rest.

You can't think your way to this, so if you're trying to do it from your head, stop and surrender your mind into the ultra-connective state. Be with Life all around you and then allow yourself to be who you really are!

3. This is just the first step ... you as who you really are. This isn't necessarily your beyond self YOU. So here we go ... I know these are big leaps into the great unknown, but you can do it and have fun becoming it! Surrender this newest, greatest, most amazing YOU that you've always been. Yes, let it go even though you've just remade its re-acquaintance. Be willing to step into a brand new, evolving beingness that is outside the design of individuality, separation, disconnection and polarity. Step into the new collective beingness where you'll discover an ever evolving, super creational brand new YOU / US in every moment! Feel it, sense it, become it. Discover the beyond self YOU!

4. If you have any difficulty with this, try this simple exercise. We did this earlier, but play with it again now to see where it leads you. Take a deep breath and from your centre point, allow your awareness to expand to be bigger than the world. Picture yourself out in space looking at this gorgeous planet. How does that feel? Freer? Lighter? Remember, this is still you looking at the Earth. So next, allow yourself to be as big as the cosmos and once you've got that, then simply slide your awareness beyond that to touch other cosmoses beyond our own. As you complete this last step, becoming as big as the cosmos and beyond, you will discover the beyond self YOU, no longer limited by human thinking and conditioning. Here unlimited possibilities abound, waiting for us to reach for them and bring them alive. Here you'll surprisingly discover yourself feeling more PRESENT than ever before. You might suddenly hear the birds sing when you hadn't noticed them before, or the rustle of the wind, or even the wonder of the silence that surrounds you. In our new connective energetic, expanding from your centre into 'way out there' will actually return you more fully present to the here and now.

If you're feeling adventurous, you can completely let go of yourself to discover that in the surrender resides the wondrous, uniquely magnificent, new, beyond self YOU / US. Living beyond self is a liberation ... a complete redesign of beingness and all that it affords. Beyond self, you step into a new energetic blueprint of beingness sourced from an explosive new Life source ... a continuous, creational becoming that allows us to discover, within ourselves and others, new dimensions of leadership and power.

Are you ready to explore the 'beyond self' territory even more? If yes, here are some simple guidelines that can take you into the new paradigm, beyond self, living as a new visionary:

1. Open up, inside and out and in every aspect.

2. Look at the world every day with fresh new eyes and see what's possible today that might not have been yesterday.

3. Consider that you are not who you always thought you were. Be willing to surrender and let go of any preconceived notions about yourself, your abilities and your capacity to create the NEW.

4. Let passion and vision flood you. Take the energy of them into every cell and be willing to live as and for all that you can be and all that we can be.

5. Connect with creation and bring it alive in you.

6. Connect with the new Life source energy and let it source everything you do.

7. Focus on breakthroughs for Life, living beyond self, discovering the wondrous playgrounds of collective creation. 'Beyond self' living provides an incredible access to living uniquely as ALL with a lot more energy and creational power.

8. Free think. Discover that there is no truth about anything. There's only what we're willing to perceive as possible.

9. Question everything that is. There's always a better way if you're willing to be open to it and call the energy of it present and alive.

10. See beyond the moment. Look into the future of where this next choice / creation will lead you and us. Is this the best we can do now for the evolution of ALL / everything? If you simply ask the question, you'll find new insights and offerings that weren't available to you before.

11. See the world as an omni-dimensional playground and discover the brilliant transformative nature of living as and for ALL.

12. Be willing to take on BIG, BIGGER AND HUMUNGOUS visions and be unafraid to live as that in every way. You'll discover that every word out of your mouth, every sentence that types through your fingers and everything that you do will bring Life more fully alive.

13. Be willing to invent yourself anew each and every day. Discover an evolving YOU right alongside of an evolving US.

14. Dance in the new collective energetics and discover the ease and vitality of the evolution of our being.

Being a new visionary is great fun. Don't let the language, or your thoughts or concerns about taking this step beyond self, daunt you in any way. Take the leap. Play with the possibilities. Discover the world beyond polarity, beyond self that offers us the richness of ALL / everything. This is the liberation of human being, the evolution of our world and much, much more! Now who wouldn't want to be a part of all that?!!

NEW VISIONARY #6
ANNIMAC from Australia
Intuitive Futurist
www.annimac.com.au

Let's meet our sixth new visionary who beautifully personifies living beyond self. I first met Annimac on our world tour in 2003 and I have to say that meeting Annimac was one of the highlights of the trip. This is a woman who, all her life, has stood for the NEW, spoken for the NEW and created the NEW!

To list just a few of her creations over the past years:

- In 1972 she was instrumental in creating Australia's first alternative, child-centred primary school where the children ran the school themselves through a parliamentary system. Five schools were established and three are still operating today.
- In the 1980's, she set up a course in Entrepreneurship, which grew into an institute that supports entrepreneurs in Western Australia.
- She assisted with the establishment of the Fremantle Education Centre, the first federally funded centre supporting students, teachers, parents and communities in receiving education beyond that offered by traditional, mainstream education.
- She amalgamated two public media organisations into a film and television institute that was instrumental in establishing the Young Film Makers Festival that still exists today.
- She co-created the first privately owned drama film production company in Western Australia, which then created the world's first Film Deed in Law, underpinning all film investment prospectuses world-wide.
- As an intuitive futurist, she engages with corporations as well as people in government and education to encourage them in designing futures for a brighter, more creative world.

57

This is a very short list of her actual accomplishments towards the design of a completely new world. She's a change agent extraordinaire, being heard to say that 'resisting change is like holding your breath ... if you succeed, you die.' Annimac is an incredible woman, one I'm very proud to call a friend and a collaborative new visionary in this world. Here's what she has to say about herself as a new visionary and about new leadership:

BEING ME TO THE MAX

"In all that I do, I'm just being me to the max. Being a new visionary is about living as all that you are and at the same time living beyond self. You get totally focused and centred on who you are and then you never have to notice it or pay any attention to it. You disappear and you're everything at the same time. It's not self-negating or self-sacrificing. It's not about ignoring self or pushing self aside. It's the heart and essence of being a visionary leader ... to know who you are and to thoroughly be it. Once you're clear who you are and what your favourite bits of yourself are, then you simply be those to the max! The thing I most love to do is laugh. I cherish my memories of laughter. It's fundamental to our very nature to create. You thoroughly enjoy being yourself and this creates the energy that brings the visions alive.

THE INNOVATIVE EDGE

I always discover myself at the innovative edge ... the edge of creating things that haven't been before. Actually, I'm only visionary relative to other people, not to myself. I'm just being me to the max and having a great time doing it. Some people love living with the past (e.g. old houses, antiques), while others are modernists living firmly in the present. Modernists love the newest of the new ... new homes and new technology. But living in the now isn't necessarily what makes up a visionary or futurist.

A futurist lives truly in the future as a kind of non-tangible energy. Their now is other people's futures. It's why parallel universes are so great. I'm in the now, but I'm not bound by that now. Futurists are creating that now, whereas modernists cherish and live in the now. I'm always moving on from the current now to the newest possibilities. As a futurist, I need immense diversity, eclecticism and freedom for change. A visionary is always going beyond! Change is a consequence of being a visionary. It's not its purpose. If one universe is connected to another, things will be happening that create change in another. My purpose in life is to live me to the max and that will drive change. People in the now will run with the change, but they're not necessarily generating it. Visionaries actually create the energy that creates the change. As a visionary I find that I fall easily and naturally into parallel universes. Being aware that parallel universes exist and that I'm constantly moving through them, gives me a great sense of freedom to create.

WHAT YOU BELIEVE, YOU WILL MAKE HAPPEN

Part of being a new visionary is that you know that what you believe, you will make happen. It never enters my head that anything negative could happen. For example, I've never in my life been fearful of dying. I've been in near plane crashes and I just knew I wasn't going to die. Therefore I had the freedom to enjoy the experience. It's part of living me to the max. If things go wrong and seem life threatening, I believe that they'll go right and they always do. You live inside your own belief and that creates the reality.

My concept of creating or innovating something is that it has to have its own energy separate from me. I put my energy into it, but it has to have its own identity and energy in order for it to thrive and evolve. I want the creative vision to have its own momentum, so I create the energy that other people are going to run with. As a new visionary, you don't own that creation. It must evolve beyond what you, as the creator or innovator, can vision it to be.

For me, it's not about leading in the traditional ways. I have more freedom to create if I'm not well known. As a silent visionary terrorist, I can get in and out fast to create change. I can be me to the max, operating beyond self, creating what is waiting to be created. What's really exciting at the moment is that more and more people are beginning to live like this ... really being themselves more than ever before. They're nurturing themselves to be visionary leaders and that's the evolution of society."

NEW DIMENSIONS OF
POWER, LEADERSHIP AND VISION

As we enter the 'beyond self' territory, we discover even newer dimensions and levels of power, leadership and vision beyond what we've already looked at. Let's explore this new dimensionality and see where it leads us. You'll be amazed at the constant evolutionary nature of everything once you learn to watch for and co-create its emergence.

In the past, we've thought of leadership and power inside old paradigm frameworks with associated beliefs something like ......

- Power corrupts.
- Leadership is burdensome and carries heavy responsibility.
- Only one person can lead at a time.

These are untruths made up from the fabric of our cultural heritage, someone else's very old realities. So let's look at these beliefs in the light of day today and see what's so.

Power corrupts:
Power corrupts only when it's contained within a closed energy system. Once you're fully open and flowing, the energy of power moves right on through to do its creational work and you are in a dance with its potential to create wondrous things for all. As a connective being, you find it literally impossible to conceive of doing anything harmful with power to anything or anyone.

Leadership is burdensome and carries heavy responsibility:
Leadership on your own, trying to change what is, is like pushing an elephant up hill. But leaderfulness, shared in the brilliance of the moment, working with the potential of what wants to get created from all of the unique passions and expressions is such fun that the elephant sprouts wings, transforms itself and flies beyond the hill top you were originally striving for. It surprises you with its leaps and bounds, taking you on a journey of magical discovery.

Only one person can lead at a time:

Clearly it isn't true that only one person can lead at a time. That was only so in the hierarchical structure created inside closed and disconnected energy systems. Today that's all changed and a new paradigm of leaderfulness is bursting through. New visionaries know that this is their playground of choice for the world of their visions.

NEW DIMENSIONS OF POWER

So what are these new dimensions of 'beyond self' power, leadership and vision then? Let's start with the levels of power and discover how they're evolving:

Power over / powerless

'Power over' is practically the only kind of power our world has known. In fact, 'power over' is inherently understood in the very word power these days. 'Power over' tends to be the domination of personal or financial power or the power of authority to control or decide for others how life is going to go. Anyone not using 'power over' has tended to feel powerless. Hence we have lived, up until recently, in a world where we've bought into the belief that 'one person can't make a difference.' As a result, people have not fully used their individual or collective voices to stir the fires of change. They've been walking in to work everyday offering up their power to the company and its hierarchical power structure.

Soft power

As we opened up our hearts, we reached for a new kind of power ... soft power that doesn't control in any way, but in fact has its foundations in love, forgiveness, peace and compassion. With soft power, people try to be more understanding and more open to other ways of working things out.

Vibrant, creative power

As we move into the integration of wholeness, we discover the dynamic, vibrant power of creation. As we seek new ways of doing what has never been done before, possibilities come alive. Realising that everything can be made anew, we stop trying to push, cajole or love the elephant up the hill. We breathe the fire of transformation into it to light up new pathways forward for us all. About six years ago sociologist Paul Ray and psychologist Sherry Anderson identified a newly emerging social trend called 'cultural creatives' ... people all over the world creating everything anew ... home schooling, recycling, new communities, etc. In their book, 'The Cultural Creatives: How 50 Million People Are Changing the World', they identified that these creatives didn't know that there were others, like themselves, doing the same. We were a silent, but growing minority of creationalists around the world bringing in the NEW. Today, cultural creatives are estimated to exceed 150 million people in the US and Europe alone. For certain, we are no longer silent and no longer alone. Cultural creatives are new visionaries, utilising vibrant, creative power to achieve their dreams and desires.

Transformative, collective, Life source power
What, there's more? There sure is. New visionaries are stepping beyond vibrant power into alchemical, transformative, collective power. This new power works with the full power of Life source energy for evolutionary potential for ALL. It's here that we move beyond self into an evolving dimension of power that offers magical living and transformational being. Transformative power takes the energetic potential of power beyond our own personal power and amps it up into a new collective power that is available for the good of Life. If you try to misuse this power, the energy will move away from you. Why? Because there's an in-built design for Life associated with this power ... so when you're connected with it, you simply cannot conceive of doing harm to any living thing. In fact, you live so wonderfully connected that you can only do that which will empower Life in its fullest.

Transformative, alchemical power is 'beyond self' power. It operates beyond dimensionality and beyond time, space and form. As a transformative, alchemical being, you begin to see the true potentiality of people, places, situations and things. As you see people this way, so they are immediately transformed into that which they truly are ... amazing beings with incredible contribution to make.

New visionaries understand the alchemical nature of seeing the world, not as it is known, but as we create it to be. This is much more than simply being responsible for the reality that each of us individually creates. It's about standing as and for ALL, dancing with creational Life source power and living into existence a new reality for the world. The energetics are the key here as we move from our personal energy field creating our own personal reality … to operating as the energy field of the whole co-creating realities as potential and possibilities. As we perceive and live from this much vaster, collective energy field, so the bigger reality is created.

It's also hugely important to stop buying into how others say the world is and to live as if you are creating it anew in every moment, because you are. Once you're living beyond self, walking as the vaster collective energy field, then whatever you choose to perceive immediately creates the current 'now' reality.

New visionaries understand that perception is a shifting dance of creation … that there is no truth, no right or wrong, no black or white, no good or evil. There is only the way we choose to perceive things. When we can unlock the dimensional doorways from fixed time, space and form, we discover that perception is an omni-dimensional lens through which we can create our world.

Let's use an example to see how perception can liberate our ability to create. Is the current state of political leadership in the world:

- a complete and utter mess with the kingpins of power determining the demise of the Earth and all we hold dear?
- an old paradigm of power beginning to move into decline as its time comes to an end?
- the contribution of great, amazing beings who've chosen a challenging and final role to show us just how bad things can be when we choose individuality, self-focus and competition over Life?
- a signal to the new visionaries to go for it with the creation of the NEW?
- an iconic sign that we must all step into our creational power now and choose Life for our world?

Can you see that any and all of these can be a 'right' answer, depending on your viewpoint, if there is such thing as a right answer anymore? So when you look at these options above, which one(s) make you feel empowered to create movement towards greater leadership for the world now?

As a new visionary, whichever perceptions you select, be sure to choose the ones that ……

- expand the possibilities,
- open up new horizons and
- leave you and others feeling liberated and empowered to take the next steps for us all.

New visionaries look beyond the current shape of things (FORM), beyond the past and beyond the present moment of what is (TIME) as well as beyond our current worldview of things (SPACE), moving themselves beyond 3D reality into an omni-dimensional view of how things can be. Then they create from there. In fact, it wouldn't be at all amiss to say that new visionaries are cosmic in their vantage points. They know that what they vision and bring alive is touching Life everywhere. That might sound a bit weird to old paradigm leadership ears, but to a new visionary, this is a natural next step in the evolution of our leadership accountability ... not just global stewardship, but cosmic and beyond.

NEW VISIONARY #7
SANTARI GREEN from the UK
Tapping Collective Power
www.Imagi-Callity.com
www.newvisionaries.net

Santari has been my husband and evolutionary partner for the last ten years. When we met, we agreed that we were together for the evolutionary work that we could create in the world. Our relationship is based fully on that dance and it makes for one of the most liberating relationships I've ever seen.

He's an amazing man. In the ten years I've known him, I've seen him alter the face of consciousness and reality in this world by ......

- going into the garden for days, doing only what he wanted to do, bringing the liberation of passion to working life,
- writing a sci-fi fantasy about sourcing the true place of magic, bringing magical living amazingly present around the world,
- singing the powerful essence of people from the deepest place, bringing them fully alive and into themselves to be all they can be,
- being attacked by a cow and then spending two full days in bed altering his and our collective relationship to physicality, bringing a new ability to transform cells, bruises, etc. into a perfectional new state and
- going in to his office on his own and coming out in yet another new level of leadership and power, which I then see available in others within days / months of him creating it for himself and for all.

These are just a few of the examples of my husband, the new visionary. I am proud to say that he's in my life, and I'm even prouder to say that I'm sharing this evolutionary mega shift for this world with him. I give you Santari Green, magicaliser extraordinaire!

LIVING THE LIFE OF AN EVOLUTIONARY BEING

"When I first met Soleira, I was intrigued by what she told me of the man that she was looking for to fulfil an evolutionary partnership. I thought that it would be an exciting adventure and I said to myself 'I can do this, I can be that man.' The man that I then became was in connection with so many different realities, moving from one to the other, that I very quickly found myself liberated, no longer trapped in a 3D version of reality. I began to understand what it was like living in other worlds and why people come to this world to effect changes. It was as if I could see the very mechanics by which Life could be made new, fresh and exciting. So I started to embody that feeling of being able to change anything that I touched and I started to live the life of an evolutionary being.

Sometimes I would have glimpses of what life could be like if everybody lived the way that I lived. And one day I decided that I was no longer willing to wait years for that world to arrive. I decided I wanted it now. The world that I had seen in visions has arrived and new versions of it are continually occurring. People are finding their place in this greater world vision with me. I don't think it's a single vision. I think it's a collective vision that I've drawn upon from many different places and not just of Earth. I don't feel constricted to life on this planet. It feels like my consciousness is also in other worlds and other places and yet I'm very present and here. My purpose is to bring what I'm working on in these other places to be assembled here.

I love taking people beyond the boundaries so that they can find another meaning and purpose to why they're here, to why they're alive. They can really only make that type of step when they know there's something else to go for, when they see someone else living a life quite different from themselves that is so very expressive, rich and powerful. If people have these experiences, then they no longer have to ask the same questions over and over.

There are times when I know that I'm the forerunner for many different things, things that people haven't even yet thought of and have no consciousness about. But if I bring my awareness to the visions that I have, I know that people will start to have a way of connecting with those visions that can alter life for everyone, not just for themselves. It's what I believe about myself and the things that I do that allow power to emerge. In a sense I create my own access to power and I create an evolutionary context for all the things that I do.

My vision at the moment is like a feeling, where everybody knows each other so intimately that there can only be openness, respect, recognition and a working together of the highest order. For me, this vision isn't in the far future. It's something that exists in this moment and it feels like I'm creating the space in which it will eventually occur for everybody. Sometimes it feels like I'm sending out the signal, like a transmitter. Other times it feels like I've already put the vision out into the world for other people to claim as their own. And other times it feels like it's not just my vision. Everybody has already said it's their vision.

THE POWERFUL SPRING OF POSSIBILITIES

I believe that I go to a place where vision is like a powerful spring of energy that forms itself into many possibilities. All I have to do is to look at some of those possibilities and find the ones that fit what most people want and ask for, what fits where we want to go as a race of people to create a beautiful and brilliant future. And then I work with and live that energy through the things that I say to people, that I write, from the songs that I sing and in the way that I look at people. Because what I believe in is so real, it becomes real for others also.

TAPPING COLLECTIVE POWER

I believe that we all have a commitment to create the world in the way that best benefits us. I feel that I'm using that collective commitment to effect the changes. I don't have to talk to all the people. It's like the commitment itself does the work. This is the thing about true authority. When you work from a place of true power, you carry the authority.

I recently felt what it was like when the Declaration of Independence was being drawn up. I had this feeling that really

67

moved me ... a feeling of passion, of liberation, of exultation. It's when you know that something's been done that was waiting to happen. And when you touch it, it happens. When you work this way, you don't need to get people's direct agreement because they've already agreed for certain things to happen and then people start attending to what strongly calls to them. I know consciously the moments when I can make these changes happen instantly for people. You might call it a magical power, but I prefer to call it accessing our collective power.

Collective power isn't something that's abstract. It's tangible. When you touch it, it moves you to tears. It moves you to go beyond yourself and take whatever steps are necessary to make the power available to others. With the collective power, you can be daring and bold and become whatever you need to become. And somehow, from this place of collective power, I know that I can become whatever I need to be in that moment to make everything available to people.

The thought of a personal self doesn't seem to exist for me anymore. I'd say living beyond self is a richer feeling of experiencing life because you don't have to let go of something or adopt a role or become a new person. You just naturally experience changes and learn to flow with those changes. You make a stand for what you really know needs to happen next and when you're in that place, it's not like you have to work to get people to understand what needs to change. You're so committed and assured, that whatever needs to occur is self-evident. And having taken that step you feel emboldened to continue to go further, to have this life we all want to see become a reality right now and not stay a fantasy vision for some future time. You discover that you can speed up whatever is wanting to happen, introduce new scenarios that haven't been considered yet and change the ways in which people think about themselves and what they can achieve. You discover the power and the access to make our collective vision a reality.

Sometimes it might feel like you're making all of it up. But because you're working from a collective place, you know that there's a purpose that allows you to continually create what might be the next evolutionary steps for all of us. Being a visionary is about changing patterns and not being afraid to take risks, because you know that everything you introduce is of great value and can never be wrong. It can't be wrong because it sources from the collective dream. The only thing that would ever stop any of this from happening is if you didn't think it could be real. Everything I do is real. Everything I do affects Life everywhere. And I know that Life is turning out more brilliantly in every moment because I'm willing to engage with it in this way and live it to its fullest in every moment.

I'm interested in vision, being able to see differently, further, deeper and more clearly continually. I'm exploring where that takes me and I'm finding that my ability to make things more physical isn't defined by anything that anybody else has ever done before. It's like I'm tapping into some other place that people haven't yet thought to look. And when I look there, I reach into that place and pull something through that's completely brand new. I live my life as a power of immense change and movement. And because that's what I see of myself, then evolution becomes a natural occurrence. Always I am seeking for the next movements for people to take. I look to see where they will go, not just as individuals, but as a collective, as a race. I see myself in an overseeing capacity of knowing what to do to take us to the next levels of our collective journey.

I'd say this is how it's been for the last ten years since Soleira and I met. I had an experience then of knowing that I could bring everything together so this world could be the world of our dreams. And somehow I know how everything fits. It's not something I've had to learn. It's something that I've reached for and it's come to me. So now I can own it and make our collective dreams a reality.

BEYOND THE PERSONAL
... THE EVOLUTIONARY PICTURE AND POWER
I've amalgamated and integrated so many aspects of me and beyond that I'm now more of the evolutionary picture and power than I am as me as an individual. Me as an individual is just like

a character in a book. It just represents certain aspects. Who I am now is like the author of the book. I can create whoever I need to be. I know that I don't have to be a person again. I need to have the clarity to concentrate and focus upon those things I've set my sights upon. I know how to create Life and from that place I know how to create experiences for other people to go beyond themselves.

I believe that I'm in continual touch with everybody in this world. But it's the mega potential of people that I really resonate with. There are people that I meet with whom I know that I have a relationship that exists beyond the personal. In fact it's really not a relationship, it's more like a recognition that together we can and are doing amazing work that affects all people everywhere. For example, with my friend Geo, as soon as I met him I recognised that he had this ability to bring an amazing level of power present within people. All I had to do was to engage him as the holder of that power. When he recognised that he already held the power for people on a tremendous level, then he was able to go beyond his own personal boundaries and start to claim that power and that way of working for himself and others.

In those moments, it's not really about people as individuals. It's more about the liberation of the energy of collective power within our world. People are finding that energy rising within themselves. I love meeting these key people in the collective game because they have so much leverage that it enables tremendous access to all levels of leadership to enter into people's consciousness and into their physicality. From this place, every contact can be fun and Life enhancing with little effort.

One of the things I'm at work on is the way in which people can really relate to one another and to Life. I'm bringing people's awareness and attention to these connections and energies so they can become more clearly attuned to the power and beauty of things that would otherwise be overlooked, to the power of our collective dreams being consciously created by us all into reality now."

NEW DIMENSIONS OF
POWER, LEADERSHIP AND VISION

NEW DIMENSIONS OF LEADERSHIP

Let's look at the new dimensions of leadership that coincide with these new dimensions of power:

Closed leadership
Closed leadership comes from the leader being closed to themselves, others, new ideas, potential and Life. It's all about what they want and doesn't necessarily take the greater picture into account. A closed leader is locked into self simply by the nature of their reduced energetic capacity in a closed energy system. With closed hearts, minds, spirits and souls, these leaders don't tend to take the future of the world into account. Here's where 'power over' initiates, because it's the only way they can see how to get others to do things for them. Here, they are locked completely into form (the physical self) and this is usually all they can see, sense and feel.

Open leadership
Open leaders are receptive and open to new ideas and possibilities. They consider things and are considerate. They listen more attentively and have re-oriented themselves from being self-centred to being there for others. They initiate 'open door' policies and tend to be more openhearted and open-minded. These leaders are generally better liked and respected because they're available to others to assist and facilitate them in their growth and work. Here is where soft power initiates as the elements of caring, compassion, listening, connection and co-operation begin. From a dimensional perspective, these leaders have opened up more of themselves to others, but they generally are still operating in a slightly better version of what leadership has always been.

Vibrant Leadership
Vibrant leaders are charismatic, inventive, inspiring, empowering and very creative. By the very nature of their vibrancy, they are connected to new dimensions of creativity and presence. Their vibrancy sources from their strong connection with **CREATION.**

71

They work passionately for a better world, sourced by the vibrant energy of creation. Compared to anyone who is either closed or simply open, vibrant leaders have incredible energy and are able to carry on long past when a closed or open leader would have to say stop. Vibrant leaders are in touch with a depth of themselves, others and situations that comes from a much richer approach to Life. They continuously search beyond 'what is' to discover possibilities in the playground of creation.

Evolutionary leadership

Vibrant and evolutionary leadership are where new visionaries reside. Evolutionary leaders don't just seek for higher and deeper potential to bring it real. They look beyond this world, beyond time, space and form, to see what's truly possible to be created now for a spectacular creation of the future. Evolutionary leaders aren't bound by anything that is. They don't just invent better ways of doing what already exists. They invent whole new worlds, new languages, new beingness, new everything. They see hugely BIG between the spaces of time, space and form to invent everything ANEW. Evolutionary leaders aren't like the old kind of visionaries who dreamed up new worlds and said 'this is how things might be in a few hundred years.' Evolutionary leaders birth their creations in the now to bring the hundred year possibilities alive today. Evolutionary leaders give no credence to limitations of any kind. They're alchemists extraordinaire. Need money ... they know they can alter their relationship to finance and abundance with a single breath. Need more time ... they don't live within time limits or constraints. Yes of course they have 24 hours in a day as others do, but their ability to live beyond time allows them to accomplish ten times what others might in the same amount of hours. They're alchemising time to align with their creations that are for the greater good of ALL and so everything lines up with their creations, making them easy to achieve. For evolutionary leadership and power, **CONSCIOUSNESS** has been added to the mix. Evolutionary leaders know that working in consciousness in new ways will weave incredible movement and momentum into their creations. So let's look at consciousness, what it is and how we're evolving it collectively into a new kind of connective consciousness.

72

Consciousness is the playground of sentient creation, where the fabric of Life dances with the fabric of possibility and potential. It's an omni-dimensional fabric of sentient awareness, knowledge and wisdom with sparks of creation, potential and possibilities dancing through it all. Everything that has ever been (past, present or future, this cosmos or others) is available in consciousness.

Consciousness IS beyond time, space and form and yet is very present as well. In consciousness, all things are possible. You can move through time at will. You can leap vast distances in a millisecond. You can transform yourself into anything you can dream.

There have been people playing in consciousness for aeons. So what's different about new visionaries and their current playground of consciousness? New visionaries have brought consciousness to them, rather than going 'way out there', away from the Earth and physicality. New visionaries live in the NOW moment with the passion of creation, redesigning the past, present and future, building new worlds and inventing new playgrounds of possibilities for us to live in today. They don't rely on ancient wisdoms that may have suited times past. They invent fresh new wisdoms that apply to the evolutionary potential right now. They do all this with their eyes open, their feet on the ground and smiles on their faces. We have brought consciousness alive, an omni-dimensional, ultra-present, 'living consciousness' in which new visionaries create.

In the evolutionary levels of consciousness, we discover an amazing ability to easily and naturally become ALL, to know that which is knowable and to create beyond time, space and form. It's not like meditation, where we moved out into consciousness, letting go of self to become ONE, riding the waves and frequencies of oneness. It's more about becoming the living, sentient consciousness of ALL and creating, inventing and evolving from there. In seeking oneness there tends to be a loss of self. In becoming the living consciousness, there's an ever increasingly unique expression of self as ALL.

73

Connective consciousness is evolving within this. We're connecting up to ALL / everything and to one another in brand new ways, discovering our ability to connect from the deep eternal inner, sourcing a brand new mode of connectivity for the world. Imagine the possibilities of that! A world of people ultra-connected with self, others and ALL ... evolving the fabric of creation and offering us source solutions to problems we've long been unable to resolve. Evolutionary leaders are able to bring their consciousness creations into the NOW and bring them alive easily and graciously because they dance in and as living connective consciousness. It's here that we discover the true omni-dimensional playground of new visionaries.

NEW VISIONARY #8
MARK PRIEDE from Australia
Head of Coaching, ANZ Bank

I met Mark at the International Coach Federation Conference in Norway, May 2005. Three years ago, Mark took on the coaching project that Sonia and the Breakout team had identified as having the potential to further progress ANZ's cultural transformation, and address issues on coaching and feedback that consistently appeared in staff surveys. As the Head of Coaching for ANZ Bank, Mark is one of the pioneering leaders for coaching and its transformational influence on people and organisations. As a passionate student of history, he's part of a growing cadre of evolutionary strategists who are reshaping and redesigning our world.

THE EVOLUTION OF CONSCIOUSNESS
"My vision is about the evolution of consciousness. That's what I believe I'm here to do, especially in two areas, one on the personal transformation side and the other on the corporate side given business is such a key enabler of change on the planet. I've got a very positive evolutionary view of the planet. At an extremely young age, I wanted to know everything about the world from the earliest of times right up to the present. I was passionate about

the study of history, knowing that this could give us a much greater understanding over a longer time span. Seeing the bigger picture of evolution through the eyes of history, I've discovered that evolution is not always linear, positive movement. There have always been times of revolution before there's evolution. Sensing the broader sweep of history, we don't get caught up in 'the balcony and the dance', as we call it at ANZ. In other words, if we can get up on the balcony, we can get a bigger picture of how the dance is going. We can sense what's emerging by reading the bigger patterns.

For example, the dawn of new evolution is usually preceded by fear and if you read the papers, you could be quite fearful of all the stuff that's going on at the moment. But I don't choose to see it that way. I believe that we're moving to a more collective consciousness. There's a yearning for humanity to come together in a more evolved way, to recognise that we all share one great space, planet Earth. We're beginning to break down a lot of the barriers as history evolves and at the moment, the overall trend is towards people coming together all over the world to speak and to create. Clearly, a lot of the technology supports this coming together globally. I believe that we're a universal consciousness and that we're evolving towards that, with our awareness increasing exponentially with every generation.

A NEW LEADERSHIP EMERGES

I have a strong sense of emergence at the moment. Over the last three to four years, the people I've met and some of the conversations I've been having are affirming that there's such a leadership vacuum in the world today. But that's wonderful because every time 'the system' gets stuck, someone will come in and create a bit of chaos to shake it up and a new style of leadership will emerge. I have a really positive view of the new population of leaders that are coming to the fore. The core of this new leadership is being of service to humanity and operating from a complete awareness of that. For the new leaders, the new visionaries, it's this vision that's at the core of what they do. They're not attached to power or any of the aspects of leadership in the old paradigm in the western world.

75

Personally, I like shaking things up a bit and causing a revolution. It's part of the role of the new visionary, which I think I've been since I was born, even though I've only acknowledged it in myself recently. There was a time when I wouldn't admit it because it sounds too egotistical. But it is the work I'm doing, so I can really own it and live it now.

COACHING AS THE UNIVERSE'S RESPONSE TO CONNECTION

I love my work at ANZ as Head of Coaching. I see coaching as part of the universe's response to wanting to build connections and helping to overcome some of the fear that's around at the moment. I'd also love to help other organisations commence on the transformational journey that ANZ has undertaken, again because I see business as a powerful agent for change.

I originally joined ANZ after ten years in the IT industry having decided to make a career transition to Human Resources. Shortly after completing a post graduate degree in HR, I started as an HR consultant in one of the business units. It was about three or four months into my time there when my manager said 'Hey there's this seminal project underway called Breakout and it sounds like exactly what you're looking for.' So the connection was made and I got to join the early days of ANZ's cultural transformation, working under Sonia Stojanovic. Over the next few years my passion for coaching grew and I sensed that there was an enormous opportunity to create a coaching culture at ANZ and unleash the potential of our people. Eventually I was able to get approval to establish an internal coaching practice and was appointed Head of Coaching. Initially, I didn't actually have anyone reporting to me, but at the right moment I was able to recruit two of the most amazing guys I've met in the corporate world, David and Dugald, who had this beautiful energy and potential around them. Together we have created a really strong brand around coaching in ANZ. We started off with a standard, two day coaching programme for leaders where they could come along and learn the basics of coaching to apply back to the workplace. That was our entry point and we built a range of options around that. Then we created an advanced coaching programme, getting more into coaching for meaning and purpose, which is a new thing for ANZ. It's early days on that one yet. But we've built enough around our brand now that we can actually start to dabble in things that are a little bit different. We've got a great reputation, great facilitation, great coaching and great referenceability, so it's exciting times.

COACHING AS AN ENABLER
When I started with ANZ I had a conversation with the CEO at lunch one day and I said 'How many conversations do you think take place at ANZ every day? Let's say there are 50,000 conversations. How many of those do you think, at the end of the conversation, are actually uplifting conversations as opposed to either neutral or negative? Look at the potential in all those conversations to improve people's awareness.' I saw coaching as an enabler, enabling us to connect better through conversations with the ultimate outcome of people being more energised, more enthused and with better business results. I see my role as helping to facilitate that on a broader scale. In the next year, we'll be looking to expand that beyond ANZ to build a community in Australia, working on a broader scale, evolving consciousness. Increasingly I've had conversations with Australians and people outside of Australia that affirm my own views of the world and how it's changing. I'm finding more and more like-minded people, more new visionaries if you will. I'm so lucky to work for an organisation where we can have some of these amazing, transformational conversations. None of us would have believed ten years ago the kind of conversations that are now going on inside the corporate world.

A GLOBAL VISION
One of my dreams, the grander vision if you will, is to be working with a network of like-minded people and organisations throughout the world, coming together where there's a need identified for greater purpose to share connections, resources, ideas, etc. I love putting people in touch with one another. You never know what will eventuate from the synergy of these connections and from the transformational conversations that create evolution."

77

NEW DIMENSIONS OF
POWER, LEADERSHIP AND VISION

NEW DIMENSIONS OF VISION

We've seen how power and leadership are affected by evolving dimensionality and consciousness, now how about vision? Is vision changing as well in this new omni-dimensional paradigm? It is!

Personal Vision / Goals
Personal vision is about what you want for you and yours. It's generally focused around self. In third dimensional reality, there are many people who live without vision of any form in their lives or if they do have vision, it's more likely in the form of a goal ... a single thing to strive for next as an improvement to what is currently available to that person. Here, for example, a person might say 'I have a goal to improve my education, so I'm going back to school to learn more.' The goal is likely to be a well-rounded individual with a better job and more income.

Singular visions
As people begin to open up, they get more in touch with their desire to make a difference, to do something greater with their own gifts and abilities. They reach out to do something for others. Here vision generally comes to them in a singular format. In other words, they perceive that they can only take on one big vision at a time, so using our example of education, they might say, 'I stand for improving the current education system.' Now most would say that's a pretty big vision. But actually, if you look at it in a fuller way, it's about trying to change what is, which is never easy, and it only touches one aspect of Life, in this case education.

Visionary
A visionary sees beyond what is and mixes in the dimension of creation. So instead of designing their visions to change what is, they look into what's possible and invent brand new ways of doing things, which brings ease and grace to the whole process. So in our example, a visionary might say 'We're evolving our intelligence and therefore I stand for the evolution of education to take into account

brand new ways of learning and growth.' This visionary looks beyond the current education system and begins to see how we might reinvent it all based on our evolving intelligence.

Living Vision
New visionaries work in and as living vision. They can't settle onto a singular vision because they see potential everywhere exploding into new possibilities. They're working in a super-creative, hyper-speed, multi-faceted, ultra-connected space and generally don't want to slow themselves down to work on one single vision. If they do, they literally miss the boat on all kinds of opportunities, synergies and synchronicities that can make the living vision expand in all kinds of directions. So using our example, a new visionary working as living vision might say 'I am the evolutionary consciousness of living and learning. I bring the living vision of our evolving intelligence and beingness to everything I touch ... new business, education, politics, global connection, technology, science, quantum physics, etc.' As a result, their achievements far exceed those who are trying to be more focused and more singular in their endeavours. New visionaries dive into the wondrous dance of transformative living. They know that as they bring the vibrant energy of new Life source and the transformative touch to all that they do, that everything is evolved simply by the very nature of them being it and living it into reality.

Let's take an overall look at this new dimensionality of power, leadership and vision compared to the old, middle and new paradigm approaches. Referring back to the original chart on the paradigms, you'll see that our look into dimensionality has offered us a fourth option with consciousness and omni-dimensionality added into the mix, taking us beyond self. Let's call this the Omni or Evolutionary paradigm where ......

- creational power becomes transformative, alchemical, collective power,
- vibrant leadership becomes evolutionary leadership and
- new visionaries live 24/7 as living vision.

THE FOURTH PARADIGM

PARADIGM		DIMENSIONAL ELEMENTS	LEADERSHIP POWER & VISION
OLD 3D		Time, space & form Closed & separated Small self	Closed Power over Personal goals
MIDDLE Spiritual		Open heart Love & compassion Higher self / spirit	Open Soft power Singular visions
NEW Vibrant		Wholeness Creational Vibrant self	Vibrant Creative power Visionary
OMNI Evolutionary		Collective / ALL Consciousness Beyond self	Evolutionary Transformative power Living vision

In the first three paradigms, we're still human beings oriented around self, taking ourselves to new levels of human beingness. In the evolutionary paradigm, we've moved beyond the next steps for human beings to the wondrous creation of new beingness.
We enter the realm of evolution. Unfettered at last from millennia of human history and precepts that we don't even realise are filling the fabric of our thoughts and creations, we can finally stand free in unlimited possibilities, beyond self, beyond human being ... reinventing ourselves anew!

This is what evolutionary leadership and new visionaries are all about ... the evolution of being and the connective culture in which we take an adventuresome leap into the omni paradigm of evolutionary leadership, transformative power and living vision.

NEW VISIONARY #9
DIANNE KIPP from the USA
Dream Maker & Courageous Living Coach

Dianne is a magnificent dreamer and dream maker. She knows how to reach into the place of visions and bring dreams alive. She has lived and is living an amazingly courageous life, full of the magic that most people only dream of. After a long list of visionary careers and entrepreneurial businesses, she's now working as a courageous living coach to empower others to do the same.

"I welcome vision into my life and into the lives of others. It doesn't matter how outrageous the dream might be, I'm right there to help bring that dream into existence by welcoming the energy that's available in the vision and using it to create physical reality. I've always been a dream maker, able to see what was out of the range of what normal people were reaching for and able to bring those visions real.

THE FORCE
I've always known that there's this awesome, powerful force that we can tap into. It's an incredible sense of light and energy that can be directed and embodied in a way that elevates your awareness and puts you in strong connection with all possible visions. The force is always there and all we have to do is be open to it and allow the visions to come rushing in. It's like riding a wave until it takes you into another wave and another and so on.

It's very clear to me now that the power of dreams and the power of visions are awesome. I have to be careful what I wish for. Our consciousness, and the overall consciousness of the universe, is very powerful. We have to be hugely conscious of what we're putting out there and what we can expect in return.

I love visioning. Every day I find new versions of what my visions can look like, and what my clients' visions can look like as well. It comes very strongly to me with words and energy. Sometimes the most difficult part is figuring out a way to bring that into reality without overwhelming the people around me. I get the sense that they kind of look at me like 'Do you ever sleep?' or 'Do you ever stop creating?'

CREATING AND LIVING THE DREAM

I can remember as a child knowing that there was a whole lot more than the family or town I grew up in. No one in my family had gone away from there, but I just knew there was this whole world of possibility. I imagined a whole new existence for myself in another location and that's exactly what happened. I went away to school and while I was there, I was never sidetracked from what I was going to accomplish. I knew before I finished my nurses training that nursing would only be a small part of my profession and my career. I saw an unfolding of me experiencing other cultures both inside and outside the US and I no sooner saw it than it began to happen for me.

I found myself working in a large pharmaceutical company as Director of Advanced Technologies, using my nursing, research and IT background to work with strategic planning, breakthrough thinking, team building and organisational development strategy. I was a mover and a shaker on the leading edge, prompting our team to be visionary by doing things like taking them on outward bound sailing adventures, teaching them to seek adventure and creation in life. I did a whole day session with our department of one hundred and twenty people called 'Envisioning Our Future' where I laid down bits of movies with music in the background to get them to let go of what we were currently doing so that we could free ourselves and envision what the future of life might look like. We did it. We pulled it off. It completely changed our corporation's view of who the IT Department was. 'We can't do it' and 'we never do it' had been a big black hole for money in our department and that changed to 'we are the team that can and we will link our strategic technology to your strategic intention and make a huge success.'

It was while I was in this job that I began to dream into existence my next adventure ... a women's golf business ... teaching executive women how to enter the world of golf without all the rhetoric and traditional male influence of 'you don't belong here.'

82

I imagined the game of golf as a beautiful metaphor for life and saw that I could engage these women in golf as an extension of their own existence in the universal walk of life. This new venture came as easily as my dreams naturally do. Initially I was working at my corporate job during the week and doing my golf seminars at the golf course on the weekends. Every day after work, I'd make five phone calls to connect me into the world of golf and all the opportunities that I could see coming. I answered the phone one day and the person on the other end of the phone asked me if I would like to lease the driving range for a dollar a year. So I went right into my president's office and quit my job. The next day I was driving the tractor on that property, doing what it was I had to do to make my vision real.

I had always wanted to be a jock, so for four years, I did nothing but play golf, improve my own golf game, teach others golf and continue going for the PGA credential. And then one day, a new vision began to emerge. It dawned on me that it was time to do something even more creative with my life. So I became a lobbyist for the Heart Association to get the smoking cessation ban passed in Florida. This one was all about consciousness and that was great work. But again, and as always, I kept being led into the next new visions and dreams for my life.

THE COURAGEOUS ADVENTURE

For me, being a visionary means being open to any and all possibilities that exist in any moment. As soon as one possibility is gone in that moment, we're on to another moment. There isn't necessarily a need to complete things in the old traditional way or to stay in one job for your life. It's ever unfolding. It's a courageous adventure. It's evolutionary.

So off I went into the next vision and the next thing I know I've created a dream I'd had since I was a kid of owning my own sail boat and a charter sailing business in the Caribbean. I wanted to be able to take people on my sail boat anywhere they wanted to go, to snorkel and teach them about fish. Again, suddenly there it was … the opportunity was right in front of me and I found myself on this wonderful boat with a business partner.

83

Every day someone would get on that boat saying 'How did you know this was what you wanted to do?' It was wonderful to be in the water every day, helping people see what beautiful creation there was in the oceans. The sailing was magnificent and I loved my life the whole year that I spent on the boat.

After a year in the Caribbean, I began to feel a calling and longing to come back to the US to do what I'd been saying for a lot of years that I wanted to do. I didn't know it was going to be called Life Coaching because that's not what I thought it was. I didn't realise that's what it was called until I got back.

I have a vision now for my coaching business to be a coaching business clearing house, for excellence in coaching and really being able to match up the right coaches with the right clients, be they individuals, corporations or politicians. One of my penchants is to increase compassion with our political leaders. I am often heard to say that I'm creating a new kind of compassion in the universe for ourselves, others and the planet.

In my work with individuals and small businesses I invite them, through visioning exercises, to really get in touch with what contribution is in their hearts and souls, whether that's from the individual or greater perspective. I have them get clear on who they are in their being and what attributes they want to contribute to others ... their loyalty, lovingness, integrity, etc.

The next level is to get them, as a team, group or organisation, to identify what is the grand vision of the organisation and what's the most strategic intention that they can envision for themselves from their expansion into the future. Then I work with them to dream that into existence.

So here I am, present day, being a courageous living coach, empowering others to dream their dreams into reality. My own vision now is about courageous living and courageous leadership as part of the evolution of coaching and leadership for the planet.

VISIONARY LEADERS

In my previous careers, I used to think that I worked for visionary leaders. In their time they were. But the confines of their big visions had to do with physical reality in terms of time and money and physical aspects of bringing things into reality. They didn't allow themselves the creativity that is afforded when you can let go of self imposed limitations, of not enough time, of not enough money and really go for it.

If you look at some of the new complexity and chaos theory around organisational development, it really is the same. It's saying take the shackles off. More than just thinking outside the box, look at what already exists and use the energy, positive or negative. Allow it and see what comes from it. It's the understanding that energy and matter are all the same. Things that we have in physical reality are the result of our ability to congeal energy into what it is we want to see.

New leaders, new visionaries, have the ability to do this. They can tap into our connection, our awareness and our consciousness of how we are all part of the same and work with the energy to bring it alive and real. I want to say to people who are becoming new visionaries to let it flow. You could be very afraid, but no … be very open and allow the knowing that comes from pure vision. This place of pure vision is sitting there just waiting for us to tap into it to harness the energy of the vision and make it real. We can bring into reality what it is we truly want by calling on the energy and moving it towards our goals.

I leave tomorrow for this island in Maine to look at buying property that I've been dreaming about for 22 years. I plan to figure out a way to buy it even though I may not have the money for it yet. I'm going to set up a retreat centre on this property that I'll do courageous living and courageous leadership coaching and training from. I also plan to have places in Venezuela, Florida, Maine and who knows where else, because I will be living in other cultures. I'm a global being in a time of huge visionary change and I plan to play my part in this change with great abandon, courageously inspiring as many others as I can to do the same."

BECOMING THE LIVING VISION

FROM LINEAR VISION TO LIVING VISION

Coaching and strategic visioning has, in the past, revolved around individuals or organisations getting in touch with a single vision that guides and directs the efforts of the individuals and those they're involved with towards a common goal. Many have felt leadership and vision to be burdensome things to carry and therefore many people have tended to shy away from taking on bigger, let alone multiple visions. And of course, there's the old paradigm concept that vision and profit don't mix ... which is absolutely crazy. Vision, vibrancy, vitality and the subsequent abundance that comes from these is so apparent that it's crazy to think otherwise.

In addition to all that, much of our traditional 'success' teachings today would say that you should focus on one single project, vision or goal at a time; that focusing on too many things can create chaos and pressure. That might be true from an old or middle paradigm perspective, but it's definitely not true from the new and evolutionary paradigms of reality. Many energetically aware and connected people work in what I call **'vibrant multiplicity'**, the ability to dance with many things at a time. In fact, for these people, holding back the overflowing energy of passion and vision to apply it to a single project or vision tends to detract from the flow, magic and creation of the bigger picture vision occurring naturally, synergistically and synchronistically. Operating fully and completely within living vision is what calls amazing energy, magical invention and unprecedented resources to aid in the gracious fulfilment of what we can envision on the biggest scale.

Moving from linear or singular vision to living vision is about the scale of the visions we're willing to undertake and the energetics associated with that. New visionaries live all the time as evolutionary vision unfolding itself into every area of Life. They don't just tackle one big vision or project. They vision everything as how it can be from an unlimited and interconnected place, evolving it delightfully, playfully and collaboratively into what it truly can be. They know that it's all part of a bigger picture unfolding and they engage with it playfully on the big picture level. Shifting from vision to living vision is simply about moving from working only with our own individual energy to becoming the bigger, vaster, richer energy fields of evolutionary potential and connective consciousness. You literally become the greater fields in a dance with unlimited potential and possibilities.

CONNECTIVE CONSCIOUSNESS

The key to the evolutionary paradigm and the shift to living vision is CONNECTIVE CONSCIOUSNESS. If it's just you, as your own energy, trying to make something new happen in the world, it can take a long time, require a great deal of effort and be a hard slog. But if it's the 'beyond self' YOU standing in the greater fields of connective consciousness as ALL, sourcing Life, evolving evolution ... the energy, potential and possibilities are limitless.

To use an analogy, it's like the difference between a tiny trickle of a stream making its way through the forest, feeding the nearby trees and land (personal and linear vision) and a huge swirling, pulsing ocean that nurtures the world and is an incredibly huge part of our complete bio-sphere here on planet Earth (connective consciousness and living vision). Moving into connective consciousness, you're not just a drop of water in the stream, nor even the stream itself. You're the complete and total essence of water and ocean and all that it contributes to Life everywhere. So taking this analogy to its next levels, you literally become the great cosmic seas, seeding Life in all its glorious forms. This is the high vibrational, powerful, energetic experience that we get when we move into connective consciousness.

In the past, we went way out to connect with consciousness, to touch its ancient wisdoms and teachings and to become one with ALL. One'ness however, tended to have us lose ourselves in the great cosmic swirl. As a result, we'd often become less present, less stable and not want to be here anymore. But with the evolutionary advances of the past ten years, we can now live within and as connective consciousness with its pulsing, swirling, conscious awareness and movement. We literally become the whole of Life evolving itself.

Moving from the energy of self to the mega energetics of connective consciousness (beyond self) is like plugging in to a vast and vibrant energetic grid and bringing yourself more fully alive than you've ever experienced before. It's an incredible feeling and once you've experienced it, you're hooked. You wonder why everyone doesn't choose to live connected like this. It's sourceful, passionate and creative ... pulsing with new ideas, possibilities and potentials. It's not just about stepping into the field of connective consciousness and playing within it. It's about becoming it completely and totally. Every cell of you takes on the delight of the great cosmic seas swirling Life into being. And yet, here you stand, eyes open, revelling in Life all around you, stewarding the energy that can bring huge evolutionary potential alive right here, right now!

I know this could sound over the top, unbelievable and even daunting to some, but for energetically aware people, this is as natural as breathing. I've personally met thousands of people over the last ten years for whom connective consciousness is their home playground of choice and for whom planet Earth is their evolutionary purpose and passion. So whether you're a natural ALL'ist or a new beginner in the evolutionary game, here are a few simple exercises to help you find your way into the mega fields of connective consciousness and living vision. Some of these exercises we may have done earlier in the book, but it's always good to keep playing with them to see where else they might lead.

Before we start, write down your current passion and vision so that you'll have something to compare the living vision to after you've completed the steps.

UNFURLING THE NEW PARADIGM
The first step in moving through linear vision to living vision is to unfurl the evolutionary paradigm of leadership, power and vision. Understand that it is real, that leadership here works brilliantly well and that you can have the freedom to invent and create all things new. Take the step now into this new paradigm of leadership, power and vision. Just simply intend it, visualise it or imagine it and see what happens energetically as you do this. Do you feel freer and more expansive, more in touch with creation and potential?

It's in this energetic space that you'll discover the inventive space, a springboard of sorts, from which you can dive with great abandon into living vision.

LEAPING INTO THE GREAT UNKNOWN

The second step into living vision is an energetic leap into the great unknown. In the past, we've been taught to fear the unknown, to resist change and to hold steady to life as we've always known it. This is dull, dull, dull and definitely not a fulfilling way to live. Life is an adventure and the unknown is not a dark and fearsome place to be avoided at all costs. It's the playground of potential, the limitless possibilities of all that is simply waiting to be! Tune in to the seedground of potential, to the playground of creation. How does it feel? What are you experiencing as you connect with the fabric of the great, adventuresome unknown?

The unknown is rich, luscious and full of amazing things. Space isn't empty. It's full of living consciousness, potential and possibilities, just waiting for us to come play within it, to discover the wonders of a future we haven't yet dreamed.

Are you ready to take this leap into the great unknown, the seedground of potential? If you are, then go for it. Dive with great abandon and incredible glee into the fabric of creation. If you'd like, visualise it as a great cosmic sea of possibilities, of nebula, star dust and gaseous creations that light up the cosmic skies. Soar into the places and spaces where Life is unfolding itself into the next newest new. Feel yourself come alive as you let go of the concerns and worries of an old paradigm world to discover the liberation of your creational Life source power ... the high vibrational, energetic, connective power that sources movement for Life.

LIBERATING YOUR CREATIONAL LIFE SOURCE POWER

Step three is about fully liberating this power, so take another big breath and expand, both inner and outer, to access the fullness of creation. You've just done the outer expansion by diving into the great unknown. Now let's do the journey into the deep eternal inner. Take a deep breath and allow your heart and high heart (breastplate area) to open. Let your energy free flow ... pulsing and dancing its way through your body. Expand your conscious awareness to the great 'out there' and then, when you're ready, take a dive into your heart. Like Alice going down the rabbit hole, enter that beautiful solar slide within and ride it straight through the core of you into eternity on the other side. Just visualise, pretend and imagine it if it doesn't come easily to you. Picture yourself looking at the great eternal seas from deep within you. There may be a sense at some point that you've popped out of yourself and so it may not always occur completely within, but that's ok. It's a different sense of things with the deep eternal inner, a timelessness and a sense of forever that goes on and on. It's wonderful to experience the eternal in this sourceful way right from the core of you. It brings all of you more alive and present somehow. From here, you're now able to get fully in touch with the living, pulsing source of Life energy.

Take another deep breath and breathe this Life source energy up and through the core of you, pouring it out of your high heart like a fountain into the air all around you. Fill yourself and the world with this energy. How does that feel? For me, this energy has an exhilarating feel to it. It alivens every cell of you as it moves on through. If you want to enjoy this energy a while longer, please do. And when you're ready for the next step to access living vision, here we go.

BECOMING ALL
Step four is about becoming the whole of creation sourcing itself into play. Become the source of ALL / everything ... the very fabric of Life bringing itself alive. Go on, you can do it. It's fun, imaginative, playful and one of the best things you might ever do. Stop thinking this is crazy (or any other thoughts you're having about this) and enjoy the journey. See what you can discover by connecting with and becoming creation's Life source. Now, right here, poised in the moment of breathtaking, exhilarating creation, allow the living vision to fill you up. Don't think about it. That won't do you any good here at all. Let the energy of living vision flood you and pour through you. Breathe it, be it, sing it, dance it, laugh it. Do whatever it's calling you to do to integrate it into your physical being.

Then once more, take a deep breath and get into relationship with this energy. Let it speak to you. Let it fill you up with visions, ideas, creativity and invention. Let your mind soar into new horizons. Don't try to trap it by thinking 'Oh well that won't work.' or maybe something like 'The world just isn't that way and never will be.'

New visionaries FREE THINK. They allow creation and Life to flow through them, calling them to a bigger game of evolution. They're willing to discover, unfold and make real whatever Life wants to offer them next. So let creation move right through you to gift you living vision. Can you feel it pulsing through you and enveloping you in its vibrant flow? Revel in it. Delight in it. Play in it. Allow it to find its way in you. Become the living vision pulsing itself alive.

When you feel complete with this exercise, take a pen and write down a few of the ideas, visions and concepts that spontaneously came to you during it. Also evaluate your passions in this moment. Have they changed or enhanced in any way? Do you feel the call to start doing something new, different or more, and if yes, what?

Remember the vision you had before these exercises and/or before this book? How do you feel about that same vision now that you're standing in and as living vision? Has the vision changed or evolved in some way? If you accomplished your original vision faster than expected, what else would come beyond that? What other things are now passionately possible for you in the exponential vision of your ultra-connected, 'beyond self' being?

COMMITMENT TO EVOLUTION
One last step now, step five. Are you committed to playing a part in the evolution of this planet, of humanity, of the cosmos and beyond? If you are, shout YES! to the rooftops. If you're not, why not? See what thoughts (likely culturally induced) might be leading you to not want to play a part in the greatest game in the cosmoses right now. Once you've identified those thoughts, see if they're really true, and if they're not, let them go and say YES to the greatest game and to why you're really here on this glorious planet.

Once you've entered the domain of evolution from the portals of the deep eternal inner and the great, adventuresome 'out there', you'll discover the world of living vision where every day is a new adventure, of new possibilities pouring through. You'll discover that you can't touch one vision or passion without another leaping right into play. You'll move into the ultra-connected space of super-creativity where you wake up completely alive with so many ideas that you can't wait to spring out of bed to get started. New visionaries play in the living vision fields, attracting to them:

- the magic of synchronicity and synergy,
- others who share the visions and want to collaborate to make them happen and
- timeless creation where anything can be changed, created or evolved in an instant.

Transformation, creation and evolution become your every day play and the world is transformed by every single thought you have and everything you do. This is ecstatic living, sparkling with the energy of creation.

Is it this way every minute of every day for those who dance in living vision? Not always, but it's well on its way to being 100% for many of us who revel in the playgrounds of living vision. We're learning about new ways to play. We're lightening up the world, shifting it into a more gracious and dynamic place where creation thrives and connection to one another, to the Earth and to Life itself is the fabric of our interweaving global communities.

ENERGISING THE WORLD OF THE NEW
You have a choice right now. You can connect with the world as it's been or you can connect with the world of the NEW that is a vibrant, thriving reality. If you connect with the world of problems, issues, blocks, fears and general chaos and disorder, you will be giving energy to that world as our reality. The feelings you may feel from that could be despondent, despairing and, at best, you may sense a stirring within you to do something about it, if you can even imagine where to begin!

But if you choose instead to connect with the world of potential, creation and evolution, you'll discover a thriving, pulsing, high vibrational reality that is already at play in the here and now. From here, you can't wait to dive into the next invention, the next newest NEW. You have lots of great energy to take on swooping concepts of transformation with the greatest of ease. You discover that you're not alone in this new reality. Others spot your energy and your creational Life source power and they immediately want to come play with you in the living vision.

Even in this wonderful space, the 3D world still may try to overtake you every once in a while. But if you're vigilant and really ready to play in the fields of potential and creation, you'll soon discover that this is a very real, productive and passionate way to live, that Life comes easy and friends abound. Movement happens with great ease and you can accomplish more in a week or two than you might have expected to do in a year or even a lifetime.

This pulsing field of living vision is where new visionaries thrive. And they know that they're not in this field alone. Living vision is a collective field, full of others from all over the world co-creating this new reality. It's here that we enter the realm of a new, beyond self, collective state of being. But before we move further into that evolutionary exploration, let's take a look at another new visionary with living vision.

NEW VISIONARY #10
NEIL CROFTS from the UK
Founder of Authentic Business
www.authentictransformation.co.uk
www.authenticeducation.org.uk
www.sevenstages.net

Neil Crofts is the founder of Authentic Business, Authentic Guides, Authentic Transformation and upcoming in 2006, the Authentic Education Conference. His vision is a society where people are fully empowered and responsible and where there is a community of self-led people taking that kind of responsibility in every aspect. Central to the creation of all this for Neil is AUTHENTICITY. Authentic people know who they truly are, are comfortable as that in all situations and circumstances and are also comfortable with their intuitive sense of things ... all of which leads them to being responsible for the consequences of their actions. When asked what started him on this path and where it's led him, he answered:

AN INSPIRING BUSINESS MODEL
"A few years ago, after I'd left my corporate job and moved to Bath with my new partner, I was flitting through some business magazines that I'd had on subscription for many years, wondering why I never read them. I realised it was because the business model they were talking about was all about how effectively businesses could redistribute wealth from the environment to a few senior executives and shareholders. It wasn't an inspiring business model. It had no life in it. I realised that it had no meaning and with that, things just dropped into place in one instant. I should start a magazine about authentic businesses that generate their profits through the pursuit of profound and positive purpose. I've been researching and studying that ever since, evolving this vision and its concept of what business might be, what society might be and what factors contribute to that happening.

Today, Authentic Business is a newsletter that supports this vision. Authentic Guides is a community of business service professionals who share this vision and who work in a similar way.

94

Authentic Transformation is my own coaching / guiding work to help individuals and businesses to follow an authentic path, to understand what their purpose is and to be it.

Authentic business is a better way of doing business. I can see that clearly now from the research I've done around it. So now I can go into the board room of a big company and say 'If you want to make more money, then this is the way to do it ... and by the way, it's a real 'have your cake and eat it too' because you can also have meaning, love, happiness and make more money from it. By doing something that is meaningful, you have more motivation, more passion and therefore you work better and create more wealth if that's what you want.'

A COMMUNITY BASED SOCIETY

Education and business inter-relate for me in terms of the vision because I believe we're in a bit of a race against time with people doing a lot of the damage to the environment in the name of business. We need to reduce the damage that is limiting the choices for this next generation of children in order to have enough time for them to reach maturity in a society that can facilitate enlightened living. And it has to be done in a completely new way. We can learn from the past, but we are entering a completely different era and we have to be conscious of that. With environmental challenge, peaking oil resources, social disharmony, religious tensions and so on, we have to understand that it's all perfect and that we need this to propel us to the next level. Trying to fix the situation, which is the current political agenda, isn't going to lead to a solution. We need to accept the current situation, learn from it and move on to where the opportunity lies, which in my vision is a fully empowered and responsible, community based society.

Two of my key values around the achievement of this vision are self-responsibility (a non-hierarchical structure) and inclusion (the honouring of diversity). With Authentic Guides, early on there was a real push against me for not leading. I had to stand firm and say 'I'm not going to lead this. We have to work it out together.' Also there were situations of people coming into the group who didn't quite fit, who were different, causing upsets within the group. How do you deal with this situation from this vision? The conventional model is that if they don't fit in, you exclude them. But that's anti-diversity. This person is just different, so if we exclude him or her, that's a failure of community and a failure of diversity with diversity being one of our key values. In our case, we accepted as a community that we don't exclude people and once we accepted that then we could begin to work out the challenge.

BEING THE PIONEERING GUIDE

My role in all this is about being the guide. As a pioneer, I've crossed the hill and I'm looking into the next valley. I've traversed a terrain that a number of people haven't yet. In order to traverse that terrain I've had to come up with new solutions for new problems. Then I go back to the group or business or whoever and say 'Here's the terrain, here's the vision, here's where we're heading.' Then I work out and co-create with that group how we're going to cross it together. I've only traversed it on my own. I haven't brought the wagons over the terrain. So my solution isn't necessarily appropriate for the wider community. I want to co-create with the community what the solution is.

AUTHENTIC EDUCATION

That's the principal behind the Authentic Education Conference where we'll be doing it primarily in open space without an agenda or key note speakers, except perhaps for some children who'll express what support they'd like in preparing them for adulthood. The question this conference will seek solutions for is 'How do we prepare children for adulthood in ways that leave them open to their individuality and able to take responsibility for a more enlightened society?' We'll be focusing on creating an open framework that can shift education to be about the individual and their identity, truth and meaning ... to having education be a huge amount more personal. I can envision what bits of the solution might be, but the only way we're going to get there is if we can co-create as a wider community including parents, children, teachers, educators, business people, politicians, etc."

The Authentic Education Conference is an excellent example of a new visionary at work. Neil began with an idea and a vision of bringing people together to co-create a better way for educating our children. He put the idea out in one of his Authentic Business newsletters and received over 300 responses from people offering to help. Standing in the bigger vision, he easily found a conference organiser to take it on and in true new visionary style, he then found a large internet company to take on the sponsorship for it. Inside his vision, he sees running a competition for kids on-line asking them what they need to fulfil their potential and their future. He pictures using the kids live or on video to provide authentic feedback to the conference participants in preparation for their co-creation. This is a brilliant example of the leaderfulness of new visionaries. He's empowering the leadership of the children as well as adults who share a collective vision for authentic education.

In the past three to four years, Neil has been a key influencer in the UK in shifting business to be more socially responsible and people to be more open and authentic with themselves and others. In the coming year, it's easy to see that Neil is stepping even more fully into the living vision, extending it beyond business into other areas of life that touch us deeply. He's becoming the living vision of authenticity in all areas of life and the world is a much better place for it. He's a new dad in a wonderful new relationship with a visionary wife and two fabulous new children. His life is rich and full of the limitless possibilities that our future offers us.

THE NEW CONNECTIVE

THE EVOLUTION OF COLLECTIVE CONSCIOUSNESS

It's hard to talk about new visionaries without also talking about a new sense of connectedness and our evolving collective nature. Why? Because our ability to connect in new ways with one another and with the world, the cosmos and Life itself is what's creating the breakthrough for us into a whole different way of being together and getting things to turn out.

The problem with life on Earth, until now, has been separation, a sense of being isolated and separate from everyone and everything else. The truth is that we're not really separate; we're very interconnected and unique at the same time. We are so wondrously interconnected that there isn't a person in the world that isn't a part of you and all that you do. The concept of 'a butterfly flapping its wings and things changing on the other side of the world' is very true. But even that concept is evolving and we're discovering a brand new energetic way of connecting up.

Connective living in our new collective consciousness is an amazing place to live. What if we really are one gigantic being's evolution? What if source is asking us to play a new game, to bring the complete and wonderful evolution of source, Life, Earth and ALL into being? And yet it's not about being ONE, as much of the spiritual paradigm would say it. As we've already explored, the new energetics don't quite work in that way. It's about being deeply, passionately, vibrantly and powerfully inter-connected, each one uniquely themselves as and for the whole.

With the new children arriving and more and more people opening up every day, we're seeing a huge shift in our collective nature. Our collective consciousness has been moving away from being a murky sense of chaotic energies, almost distressful in its overall nature. As cultural creatives and new visionaries, we've spent the past decade clearing up the energetic mess and opening up the spaces of consciousness to bring through amazing possibilities, potential and vibrational frequency. We have remade ourselves, reconnecting and

98

redesigning our collective nature in a brand new way. Let's look into this evolution of connective consciousness to see where we've come from and to over the past decade:

Throughout the late 1990's, our collective journey included reaching up to touch our higher selves, learning to see beyond the traps of thoughts and beliefs to liberate knowing and fresh new wisdom. Collective consciousness became a meeting place of individuals striving for greater purpose for all.

In the early 2000's, we met on the higher planes of consciousness to design the new reality in which we wanted to live. Collective consciousness became a higher, and to some degree unconscious, strategic creation of our vaster, cosmic selves.

During 2003 and 2004, we brought this design into living realisation, birthing a vibrant new reality. Once the playground was ready, we stretched our horizons to the deep eternal within, birthing a new source consciousness for the evolution of being. Collective consciousness became a holistic merging in a holographic design (each one representing the whole as a piece of the whole).
In 2005, we were learning to live as source beings, letting go of anything from the old to open up new vistas of potentiality. We expanded even further to **WHOLOGRAPHIC** consciousness (each one as the whole of the whole), discovering 'beyond self' living.

2006 is about the emergence of our new connective being ... the evolution of connective consciousness. Stepping beyond human being into the oceans of vast potential, we're co-creating the evolution of all that we can be, not just as individuals uniquely and creatively expressed, but as the whole ... living passionately, zestfully and inventively as ALL for ALL.

Today, as I write this, I would define connective consciousness as our ability to connect into and live as our collective energetic field, encompassing all the levels of our being. It's all being brought together in a transformative dance of omni-dimensional potential as a powerful energetic presence. Whew, yes I know, that's a lot of words and it might seem complex without the experience of it. So let's try it again, perhaps a bit more simplistically said this time.

Connective consciousness is an omni-dimensional collaboration of all that we are on every level.

It's the coming together of all the resources, all the forces, all the knowledge, all the beingness, all the wisdom, all the knowing and all the energies to create something magnificently brand new.

If you talk to highly aware kids today, some of them will tell you that they feel connected at any point in time to all other highly aware, super-connected kids. They're not apart or separate, nor are they one. Their collective nature is a new design, one that allows them this high level of inter-connectivity without chaos or overwhelm. They live in an ultra-connected, hypersonic, high vibrational field of resonant collective being. What's overwhelming for some of them is trying to live in the denser vibrational reality of our separate and individual selves. I mention the kids because this is part of where we, as a race, are moving to. Together, we are reinventing being from the very source of our being and redesigning Life along with it. We are evolving connective living.

NEW VISIONARIES #11 ~ THE MEGA GROUP
EVOLVING COLLECTIVE CONSCIOUSNESS

This wonderful group has been working together over the past six years, consciously evolving collective consciousness. We meet via telephone every few weeks and have done so faithfully throughout these years. We cover the UK, Canada and the USA, with all of us completely committed to taking evolution always to the next newest levels. I give you my mega buddies, the mega group, including ......

- **Trudy Zachman** (www.zachmanmassage.com) from the USA,
- **Pippa Lee** (www.lifecollege.org) from the UK,
- **Susan Friedman Kramer** (sfk9@cox.net) from the USA (who was in hospital with a neck injury working on the evolution of presence while we did this call),
- **Alice Finnamore** (www.alicef.byregion.net) from Canada and
- **Helen Rockliff** from the UK (helen@evolutionaryliving.co.uk) along with Santari and myself ......

Trudy   Pippa   Susan   Alice   Helen

Trudy: "I've been at this my whole life. As a little kid, I always knew that what was going on around me was not the real picture. People weren't walking their talk or doing the things they said they'd do. I was always interested in the things that other people weren't interested in, even as a small, small child. As an adult I began to look at things differently and wanted to be around people who looked at things with a new, independent lens. I tried out different avenues, but I was really happy when I discovered Soleira and Santari and this group. It seemed that other experiences or groups only took me so far as they didn't seem to be able to get past the current model they were working on. I have always been someone who was working on the newest new at some energetic level before it even showed up in the physical."

101

Alice: "I'm not sure what year it was, but I began to realise that I was working with other people in an energetic way in sleeping and waking dreams. I knew there was a group of souls, whether they were alive on this planet or wherever they were or what kind of beings they were, I knew there were people out there that I was connected to and doing work with. Then I got an email forwarded to me from Soleira and it just clicked with me that I had to get involved. In coming to the Global Creatives Leadership Conference in Wales that Soleira and Santari put on, I discovered that at least some of the people I was working with were actually at that conference, which was pretty cool. I discovered that I could be working with others, that I didn't even know, on an energetic and consciousness level and that that was as real as other things I was doing in physical reality in my life."

Pippa: "Throughout my whole life, I've always met the exactly right people at the right time. My life has been a fairy tale of meeting wonderful people. Through a wonderful friend and catalyst I met Soleira in the most unlikely circumstances in a caravan on the Isle of Wight, where we were both to be speakers at an event. From there began a firm friendship and I began to work with Soleira and Santari, even meeting my amazing partner, new visionary Ian Lewis, at a Corporate Soul Conference organised by them. My life is like a story, but a fantastic and beautiful one. I put my hand up a long time ago for the evolution of humanity. I believe the evolutionary leap is here. Now it's just about the rest of humanity catching up and understanding that it's happened so everyone's lives can be filled with the joy, wonder and adventure of it."

Helen: "I've always been interested in the mechanics of how things work. I had been searching up until the end of the nineties and from then, as we met and began to work consciously together, I stopped journeying and yearning and I started adventuring and exploring. Over the years I've been associated with this group, I've seen how exciting it is to create the state where all of this is accessible in an every day sort of way. My focus has been how I can bring this in to land. I'm one of the people working specifically on how do you get what's 'out there' to be liveable here in matter.

So it's been a divine to the human kind of journey rather than human to the divine.

In the past five years, as this group has worked together, I've seen a shift of frequencies to such an extent that new possibilities are available to a new matter. I've seen us working with the next level of consciousness at each stage, constantly looking at what needs to happen next and what's the shape of that. There's been a bringing together of all states, vibrancies, frequencies, levels and dimensions, so that we actually now have full access to all those things that were outside of matter and pure consciousness before. We're playing with the opportunities this is giving us to evolve things in physical matter and that's so exciting."

Pippa: "We've all been willing to play in the newest of the new and to be with whatever's next. And therefore as a group, we've moved beyond any of those old belief systems to allow whatever is truly new to come through when we work together. Other groups may not be able to do this because they hold on to a certain paradigm or structure. With us, there is no structure or framework at all, so we can really go with whatever wants to come through in the moments that we work. We all have a commitedness and a hands up'ness for that to be so and therefore it works brilliantly for us as a group."

Soleira: "That really is true about us. For example, we design a brand new level of consciousness and then wham, it's gone and we're into something completely brand new that is the evolution of that. We have to keep letting go and moving on all the time in order to continually have it evolve into more and more and more."

Helen: "It's really important to sit comfortably with the discomfort of change. In those moments where it's obvious that something's moving, it can seem personally painful and quite bewildering. That's when it's really important to keep sitting with it in the biggest way, exploring it, comparing notes, keeping in touch with one another and evolving it until we settle into a new breakthrough around it. It's the nature of our new relationship to evolution and our ability to be conscious with it."

Pippa: "Yes, and reminding each other that it's never personal whatever happens. It's always for something much bigger and far greater."

Trudy: "For me, as a person who works energetically and in consciousness, it's been wonderful to be in a situation with a group of people where the other people can understand what it is that I'm trying to articulate even when I don't necessarily have the words to describe what I'm experiencing. I'm pretty much always on the edge of stuff that most people don't even know about yet and having it brought into conscious language and understanding really helps to make it real and not just for me, but for everyone."

Alice: "I think in order to evolve things, somebody has to see it and speak it into existence. For so long, so many people have only looked at what is in front of them as possible or real. There are a lot of people who still think like that. But we've been looking at things in a completely different way, so when we see something new and we vocalise it, that makes it real and then other people can see it once it's been put out there like that. I think it's made a big difference even though it might look like it's just a few of us talking on the calls. But then we go out and live it and talk about it. Then others begin to see it as a possibility, opening their eyes to it and growing into it."

Helen: "I'm seeing the proof beginning to come home to roost. Like the evolutionary work that we did ages ago with MacDonald's and drinks companies, they're now moving to the new possibilities that we were pointing to several years ago. It's interesting to watch the various pieces of consciousness work we've done together come into realisation. We used to have to wait perhaps twelve to eighteen months before the work that we did in consciousness actually came in to land, but now we're creating and seeing the results of that almost immediately. Evolution is speeding up."

Soleira: "One of the things that we've done is to evolve consciousness to the point that it's so integrated, that it's not distinguishable as much anymore. It's woven into the fabric of myself and as a result reality creation for me is instantaneous now. I saw an interview of a quantum physicist who was saying that the gap between thinking something and it being real is huge. I thought, well that was true a few years ago, but it sure isn't true today, because I can have a subtle thought and it shows up immediately. That's part of us making it all so very real. We took consciousness from some high flying, high intellect, weirdy woowoo stuff to some very realistic, living life, practical applications, bringing it through and using it in every day life.

That's just one of this group's accomplishments over the past five years. Another is the constant evolution of collective consciousness, which we're now calling connective beingness. Do you remember back three years ago on one of our calls when there were other people in the group? The whole thing went amuck one day and the whole of the collective consciousness that we had been working on broke and we thought oh no, panic! But now I look back and I think 'oh isn't that sweet', because one of the things was that we weren't letting go fast enough. Now built into the fabric of the new evolutionists, the new visionaries, is that constant leap, leap, leap where you go searching for the leaps if they're not here because life is too dull without them."

Trudy: "We've also been evolving our relationship with physicality and well being as well. I work hands on with people every day in my practice. How I interact with them today is so different than I would have interacted with them 10 to 15 years ago. And even in my own physicality, I'm experiencing it differently. I'm more in charge of how things go, of choosing my reality and of creating my own well-being. This has been a particularly passionate interest of mine to evolve."

Helen: "Each of us has our own passionate interests, like children, relationships, business, physicality, etc. As we've become more whole and have learned to work more as a whole, the exponential factor happens. We create a kaleidoscopic effect where it isn't just one person saying how it goes. It's every person inputting their unique magnificence and contribution into the total creation and that gives us something much more exponential than anyone of us could have imagined or created on our own."

Soleira: "We've been working kaleidoscopically on the evolution of conscious being and connective consciousness. We've designed into it things like not having to get your learning through trauma, but to have everything happen with grace, ease and understanding. Or having the energy of Life source power move away from you if you're not in a good state to steward the power. These things all came from the exponential, kaleidoscopic inventions of us working together on the big picture of our conscious evolution."

Santari: "I think what's really fun about this is realising that we are the creator, the super being who is watching this whole thing unfolding and if we step into being that, then everything is perfect and fine and always has been and always will be. As a group, we've packaged together our creatorship and become the super being. It's happened because we just decided that we'd pool everything that we had together and that we wouldn't keep these separate stances of being source. That we would be a source in its totality, without limits. And we're seeing other people picking up on that idea too. Why be separate from what other people are doing when you can just share and enjoy what it is you're doing for the sheer fun of it?"

Soleira: "One of the things that I've loved about us working together is that we know that we're these conscious beings doing all this amazing work in the here and now. We could have done it a bit more airy fairy, like 'oooh look at who we are' kind of thing. But we didn't. We did in fresh, modern, fun, adventuresome, playful ways. I've had this passion to make evolution modern and new, rather than grabbing it from the past and it's been great fun playing at that with all of us together. What we've accomplished has been extraordinary and that we've done it all together so graciously, playfully and consciously in ever evolving ways is what truly makes it evolutionary. We are a wonderful example of the new conscious connective at work and play in the world."

THE NEW CONNECTIVE

CONNECTIVE LIVING

Connective living forces us to reassess our concept of how Life is. For example,

- Is the universe a dark empty space or is it a pulsing, sentient consciousness with thriving potential in every point?

- Is any human being operating completely isolated and on their own or does everything we do, see, touch and breathe create the reality for the whole?

- Is a single being a collection of molecules and particles that make up a body and mind or is a being the vast array of wondrous energies and consciousnesses that cross over dimensions and cosmoses?

- Does anything happen to us that isn't of a higher, super-conscious, collective creation?

- And what if we could live from this connective place in all that we do? How would that touch the whole if we could live as and for the collective all the time?

One might think that living as and for the whole could be a strange and disorienting experience. But in truth it's not like that. It's a full on, connective, empowering, magical Life. This is where new visionaries live and play beyond self, living as and for the whole. They live for things far greater than themselves and they measure their accomplishments not at all by standard measurable means. They measure their accomplishments on the ripples and creations in the whole, not just what appears in the moment to be the visible outcome. They know that they are inter-connected with everything and they live their lives joyfully from the power of that space.

What if we have come here all together now, in this marvellous turning point of forever, to create a brand new evolutionary future for us all? And not just for human beings and the Earth, but for Life everywhere? I know that might sound over the top to some. But if you really feel into yourself, deep inside, you may discover the place in you that knows why you've come ... and in that place you will discover our interconnection on a very profound and powerful level.

You see, we're not just another generation of human beings who are trying to solve the problems of the world. Far from it! We cross the boundaries of age, sex, race, religion, geography and even humanity, to discover ourselves as a collaboration of sourceful creators able to empower, activate, evoke and catalyse Life in evolutionary new ways.

We're not here to solve the problems. We're here to dissolve old reality by being the 'evocateurs' of something sparkling brand new. We have come en masse over four or five generations and en masse we work co-creationally. We know that it's not about any one being leading the way. It's about a collective co-creation, each one carrying very special gifts for the whole.

We know from very, very deep inside of ourselves that we're global and cosmic citizens. It's not something we have to learn or grow into. It's the very essence of who we are. We love the picture of the blue planet in space. We live in a time when we are able to see, at long last, due to technology such as the Hubble telescope, the magnificence of the cosmoses. We are in touch with Life far beyond the boundaries of Earth and its inhabitants.

Every single person has something so magnificent within them that it staggers the imagination and takes your breath away when you're able to touch it. It's not just about striving to live a better life, to provide for your family or to generate a good, safe community for your children to grow up in. We're here for mega purpose and Life-altering potential ... and new visionaries know this.

What does mega purpose and Life-altering potential look like?

- Perhaps you're the one to unlock a brilliant new way of connecting, beyond anything we've known before.

- Perhaps you're going to bring the world voice together through something like Live8.

- Perhaps you're the designer / strategist who sees the kaleidoscopic design and knows how each piece fits together into the whole.

- Perhaps you're the one to unleash the potential and contribution sitting within every single one of our amazing new children today.

- Or maybe you're the one who can unleash the god presence in every single human being in a single go.

Imagine that! A world in which every single being on the face of the planet gets to live as all they can be, contributing everything they have to give, living in full abundance and adding to the beauty of the planet as they do their work and play.

Can you see that this is way beyond anything we've known of leadership before now? This is about a whole new realm of leadership and power. It's so far removed from old leadership and power that it's almost laughable that the two can coincide in real reality. Well of course they can't and that's why we're seeing the dissolution of old leadership and power happening today and a move into the high vibrational frequencies of new reality creation.

Are you ready to become a new visionary? If yes, then look deep within yourself to touch the source place in you. Find the place in you that sings with desire and passion to create a better world and a brilliant place in an evolving cosmos. Discover there what it is you've come to gift to us all. We're co-creating a kaleidoscope of evolutionary possibilities and it will take each and every one of us to make this come fully alive.

We're no longer living isolated, separate lives, able to ignore Life around us. We're cosmic adventurers come to discover the evolvement of Life in this corner of the galaxies. We bring all manner of abilities, knowledge, connection, consciousness, wisdom and more! We dance in the creation of a magnificent future, one in which we began as human beings, tiny grains of Life on a small blue planet, to become extraordinary beings enriching Life everywhere.

When you have arrived at this place, you will find that you are no longer alone. You will discover new levels of interconnection and your part in the greatest game. You will live no longer as the small, personal you trying to get by in a world of chaos and disorder. Instead you will discover yourself as the connective collective dancing with every other living being to create a cosmos of explosive potential and vibrant, creational power. It's here that new visionaries really come in to their own, not as individual selves, but as the whole evolving itself beyond anything we've ever known.

I invite you to dive in, to hold nothing back, to surrender everything you think you are with great delight and glee to discover a world of wonder and magical creation. I invite you to step now into your own new visionary leadership and power and stun the world with your brilliant contributions. For it's here, with each one of us doing all that we came to do that we'll really discover the magnificence of evolution on the grandest scale.

NEW VISIONARY #12
JOHN BLAKEY from the UK
Group Director of Coaching, LogicaCMG
Collective Actualisation ...
Business Transforming The World

John is the Group Director of Coaching for LogicaCMG and co-founder of the strategic coaching practice, 121 partners. He is a man who truly stands for transforming the world. I've only known John for a short time, but it feels like we've known each other for a very long time. He's one of those people that sits on the edge of your consciousness, reminding you always of something bigger, something more and definitely that there's something truly glorious about this world. In the past months, I've watched him take leaps and strides as a new leader, daring to go where others might fear to tread. I love his vision for business and it's with people like him on the job, that we can be certain that things on this gorgeous planet are going to turn out just fine. I give you John Blakey, a beautiful example of a new man, embracing his masculine, feminine and visionary sides to personify and empower new business leaders who can and will change the world ......

TRANSFORMING THE PARADIGM OF LEADERSHIP

"My work in the world is to act as a catalyst for the transformation of the paradigm of leadership that has pervaded most of the world's institutions. A transformation from a masculine, intellectual and secular paradigm to one characterised by the feminine, the emotional and the spiritual. It's the field of business that I'm at work on at the moment. It's going great, but there's always a lot more to do. The good news is that the world of business has done a lot of work on itself in the past five years. Today, I'm meeting leaders who are making a difference and looking for the courage to declare who they really are and what they really stand for.

For example, yesterday I was in Oslo, Norway with a chief executive of a global company and the word spirituality came up in the discussion. We talked about it quite openly. I said 'Are you ok with this?' and he replied 'This is fantastic and brilliant. I'd really like to explore this more.' In the past, you'd struggle to have this kind of conversation in the workplace. Now it gets easier by the day. It's great to have this kind of stimulating conversation and not feel it's heretical in the world of business today.

There is a realisation that these concepts can be applied practically in business. That's what's coming together ... the practicality on the one hand and the spirituality on the other. We are realising that we can have our heads in the clouds AND keep our feet on the ground. When I use the word spirituality in business, the significance of the word is that it's a password to get into a completely different conversation around going further, going beyond the 3D world. It's a code word. It's something new that wants to happen. It leads to other words and concepts like energy, consciousness, creational power and the field of pure potential. Somehow we are part of all this and we feel it coursing through our veins. It liberates us to enter a whole new paradigm of leadership and business, pointing us to this evolutionary urge.

The vision of what business is about in the world is shifting in a more spiritually oriented era. Business has traditionally defined its vision as playing an economic role in life and I think that's no longer sufficient for ourselves or for our race. The business world is qualified to lead a different and new role with a broader vision around evolving our world as well as making money. This step will require business leaders to stand up and talk about global challenges that have not traditionally been seen as their primary agenda, issues such as war, religion, famine, sustainability and education. The courageous ones will declare their intent to have these new conversations in the traditional corridors of power. For me, this would be an example of new leadership ... a complete shift of leadership in the world driven by business leaders who have shed their need for self esteem, belonging and security and are simply driven by their inner conviction for something greater than themselves.

Business leaders can play a collective leadership role that aims for the evolution of our consciousness. Politics is too attached to the national state and religion is too attached to the beliefs from the past to be able to fulfil this role. Business spans international boundaries and has no attachment to any religious agenda or to the past. Global business leaders are free to make this leap and I believe that they can and will soon say that they are going to assume this mantle on behalf of the human race ... not just on behalf of our shareholders, employees and customers, but for everyone.

For example, take the Middle East crisis, what's going on today in Lebanon and Israel. Business leaders are not filling their 'to do' lists up with that challenge. Why not? Haven't they got anything to say on this issue? Do they think it's acceptable? The vision I live into every day is about those business leaders recognising that contributing their voice to issues such as the Middle East crisis may now be the highest manifestation of their leadership skills, by getting involved in that 'messy' world, bringing their skills, experience and inspiration to it. We need this to happen because, quite simply, those that have been traditionally responsible for these issues (politicians and religious leaders) are not solving the problem. A business leader can say 'Right, this is where we're going to focus. We're going to commit ourselves and our companies to solving a world problem.' And the great news is they can do this whilst still creating profits for their shareholders. Their staff, customers and suppliers will be so totally inspired by this vision that they will bring their whole hearts, minds and spirits to that workplace and deliver amazing results.

AN EVOLUTIONARY TURNING POINT

The backdrop to this discussion about the business world is that I believe we're at some sort of turning point, an evolutionary leap in consciousness, ready to become something new. This needs to be catalysed and tapped into ... that's the leadership role. It's about becoming role models for this leap, helping to transform fear for people. People can be frightened about what's involved in any kind of leap. If our leaders can say they're not frightened and in fact that they embrace this and are helping to co-create it wonderfully, then it helps others to make the leap with a lot more courage and power. We're at this new transition point where someone has to burst the traditional bubble and be courageous to do that on a worldly stage. I'm available and committed to playing the highest role I can in bursting bubbles or in helping others to burst that bubble. The more I say that, the more I declare myself for that, the more opportunities will come to me to fulfil that function.

THE COURAGEOUS JOURNEY

How did I get here? Well, my own journey around courage began about ten years ago when I experienced what can only be described as a revelation. For four or five days I went into an altered state of consciousness as a result of being coached. My awareness went to

113

such a level that I absolutely lost my sense of self and my personal identity. In those moments I saw everything and knew everything. It was an absolutely shattering experience in that it shattered all my belief systems. Everything I had built around ego was completely laid to nothing. I felt I needed to rebuild and find some sort of ego framework, but in the period before I did that I saw, heard and understood awesome stuff pouring through me. It was like being rewired from the core. Everything changed for me from that moment onwards and that's why I gave up my traditional leadership role to do what I do now.

But immediately after this experience I was extremely frightened about talking about it. I thought I had gone 'mad' and recognised that what I had 'seen' could be regarded as very threatening to traditional concepts of power and leadership. I had been 'the old paradigm leader' myself for many years and I knew this revelation had put me in the role of 'poacher turned gamekeeper.' It was like being a turkey and voting for Xmas, but I knew I had to work out a way to do it ... there was no alternative. So it took me three years to even talk about it to the people who were closest to me. Today I am sharing it with relative strangers, which is a measure of how far things have come.

Every step, from those three years to now, has been about sharing the experience with more people. It's been about not being ashamed of it, to say this is wonderful and it's what we all want for the world. I want to come out of the closet more and more and that's my contribution. It's finding the courage to share it, to bare it further. What I experienced wasn't a dream. It was as real as anything that ever happened to me. It inspired me to want to help people move to that point. It was joy.

Why did this 'revelation' happen to me? I think I was desperate. I'd searched in every room of the proverbial house to try to find meaning and I was desperate because every room in the house, even having been turned upside down by the considerable power of my intellect, did not yield the answer, did not yield meaning. With this experience, a new door opened to a completely different world that I didn't know existed and that world gave me a

114

profound sense of meaning. I am still in that world now and I'm in both worlds now. It's about having your head in the clouds and your feet on the ground. I had a choice. I could have left completely at that time. I honestly believed that I could have made a choice to go and that would have been fine, but I chose to stay, to share my experience and to have others be inspired by it.

BRINGING THE WORLDS TOGETHER
Recently that's been my work on myself ... reconciling that you can be in both of these worlds at the same time. I can make it one world where I do both aspects. I can tap into the absolute creative power of the universe and, at the same time, I can be John Blakey eating at McDonald's with my kids and talking about football. That's a hugely liberating concept. I didn't think I would be able to live a normal life after experiencing what I did. But instead I continue to live a normal life even as I continue to share this work.

I'm finding I have confidence to do more, to know that I don't have to hold it back. I can make a cosmic contribution while being John Blakey, normal guy with a wife and two kids. When I'm coaching a leader one to one, I know that I'm contributing to a collective movement and I'm confident in that. I don't need to be known for it or famous for it. I can just do it and be anonymous and that, for me, is a great formula. There's no ego attachment to it. I'm just doing what I'm here to do and nothing else matters. In the past I would never have said things like that. I would have been in my leadership for a worldly goal ... money, recognition or a feeling of achievement. That's what used to drive me as a leader, but it doesn't any more. I'm free of that. What drives me now is breathing, getting out of bed every morning, feeling the sun on my face, making contact with someone. Just being is what drives me now and with that, everything else looks after itself.

COLLECTIVE ACTUALISATION
I'm not sure if I can say that who I'm being is 'beyond self', but I am sure that where we're headed is 'beyond self' territory. One of the concepts established and well thought of in business is Maslow's hierarchy that builds towards self-actualisation. This was a huge visionary thing for him to create all those years ago,

but maybe a limitation on that model is the word 'self'. Maybe it's time for us to take it to collective actualisation. This is a huge, broad, collective thing, beyond the 'self' world altogether. I believe this is where we're headed ... beyond self-esteem, beyond security, beyond belonging ... to collective actualisation. I don't have the language to say what that is exactly and maybe that's not necessary. Maybe this is a space that defies conceptual, intellectual definition. I hope that I'm being it and that that will make it real in the world.

I think this comes back to me. I have to have the courage to role model it. I need to speak about it in meetings and in groups with business leaders. I have to make it part of my contribution. I don't know how many people think about it until I declare it myself. Maybe we're all thinking about it and nobody's taken the first step. I suspect on a Sunday evening they think about it and then forget about it Monday to Friday. We have to bring our whole selves to the business world. We can't leave those whole selves at the reception desk; we have to bring them to work.

For me, it's one conversation at a time. I want to have that conversation more often and with more people. I want to take a step to introduce it into the conversations that are already happening. If I do that, looking at it in a new way, I can trust that things are changing the moment I voice it. Things have already changed now. Even my sharing this has changed things. There's more curiosity and more desperation out there, similar to what drove me to experience this shift myself. I'd tried everything else and then I found what I needed to bring myself into the world of a vision that's bigger than me. Collectively, maybe we've tried everything else and it hasn't worked. We call ourselves an advanced species and there are people who believe we've achieved wonderful things and that we've come a long way. But relatively we're still crawling around on our knees with a big evolutionary leap staring us right in the eyes.

I don't know where these words will go, but whoever does read them, I want these words to nourish their souls, to help them trust themselves and to believe they do have the courage to take their

116

own next leap. Maybe there are other people out there who, like me, were very frightened about the process of speaking their full truth. But the good news is that it hasn't done me any harm and in fact it's been the most joyful experience of my life to walk this path. I hope that gives them the confidence to walk their own path and to be who they really are. It's fascinating to talk about life, vision and collective actualisation in this way. It's a privilege to have this conversation and to be a catalyst for this evolutionary shift in the world."

Swept Along & Smiling ... a poem by John Blakey

The current of our buzzing potential,
Sweeps us to a port unknown,
The stirring of our spirits,
Hints at a form to come,
Bringing new thoughts from the All,
Into this shower of mass and words,
Conjuring great creations,
Like a potter at his wheel,
And the How, the What, the Where,
Is of no import to our looming intent,
No relevance to our right brain stream,
Windows will appear, gaps and seams,
The future beams a message through this porthole of our dreams,
To the merged
To the coalesced,
To the clustered,
The chunked,
The re-formed,
The remembered spirits,
'Seize yourselves and your world today'
'In the cause of the shortening of time'
'In the cause of the acceleration'
'For the joy of our divinity expressed'
'For the rising of the blessed'
'And the loosing of Heaven's rusted gate.'

A NEW AUTHORITY AND PRESENCE

We've looked at new paradigms of power, vision and leadership and explored the collective shift into connective living. Now, let's play with evolving levels of authority and presence that are coming right along with these new paradigms:

PARADIGM		AUTHORITY	PRESENCE
OLD 3D		Hierarchical Controlling	Overbearing or No presence at all
MIDDLE Spiritual		Higher authority Touching the hem of the garment	Masters / followers It's more about others than you
NEW Vibrant		Co-creational Collaborative	All of you fully expressed and alive
OMNI Evolutionary		Cosmicious knowing Big picture seeing	Presencing presence Transformative being

It's one thing to see these words on a chart and it's quite another to actually experience the authority and presence of someone who's operating in evolutionary mode. That's as far from old paradigm leadership as you can imagine. If I could describe the levels from an energetic and experiential viewpoint, it might look and feel like this:

<u>Old paradigm authority and presence:</u> What personifies this for me is picturing a speaker on a stage with a power point presentation behind him, droning on with meaningless sentence after meaningless sentence, leaving me untouched by anything that remotely resembles inspiration for Life. We all know this one. How many times have you had to sit through some expert, CEO or leader who simply bores you witless with their old premises of life in the 3D lane? I even know of many supposed inspirational speakers who I would put in this category as well. If I don't get up off that chair shouting hurray to Life and having discovered something fantastically new that inspires me into visionary action, then I prefer not to sit down in the first place. How about you? Are you about done giving energy and time to old paradigm authority and presence in any form?

Middle paradigm authority and presence: The middle paradigm offers a soft, compassionate approach to leading. In business, this might look like a gentle leader who cares deeply about others, who is lovely to work for and who does his / her best to take care of the people they're working with. This is great, but it's not about presence and authority. It's nice to work for someone like this, but from a vibrant, visionary perspective, wouldn't you want to work for someone who calls you to something greater in yourself and who inspires excellence from you? And then of course there's the spiritual paradigm aspect of authority and presence. Hands up if you go bananas watching spiritual masters with people bowing at their feet? From an evolutionary view, every being is equally magnificent and no one who allows any other beings to place themselves subserviently lower can truly be called a master. Too often we give away our power and our own full and connected knowing to someone who is purported to be a master. This must stop now. We have discovered how to tune in to the greater intelligence and to know for ourselves what there is that's right for each of us. Authority must move from the old and middle paradigms of 'someone else has all the answers and we should follow them blindly' ... to every one of us has full access to the knowing and understanding that gifts us Life.

New paradigm authority and presence: Now here's where true inspiration really begins. Inspiration to me is something that reaches out and lights the fire of creation in others. If an inspiring speaker doesn't light that fire, then they're more about entertainment than inspiration. The authority that's in this new paradigm is fun, light and co-creative. These leaders don't assume they have all the answers. They seek to discover NEW answers by pulling the best out of every single person involved. In a new paradigm leader's presence, you feel more alive, more seen, more understood and much more in your own authority and presence.

Evolutionary paradigm authority and presence: Here's where we really discover true authority ... of a greater intelligence and of collective intent and vision. It's about the full authority of knowing on many levels of perception and understanding. It's about guiding, directing, inspiring and creating the evolutionary space for others to step into their full evolutionary authority and presence. When you experience an evolutionary paradigm leader on a stage, you will know it. You'll be jumping up and down on your chair. Your energy will be soaring and you'll be wondering how you're going sit still another moment. You will recognise your own self in them, seeing your full magnificence in the connective presence that they exude. They are presencing presence in everyone they come in touch with. They're transformative agents sparking evolution into play right here, right now. They're visionaries and big picture evolutionists and they know that since they're 'the one' at the moment who's got the vision, that it's for them to begin the dance of authoritative presencing of possibilities until everyone involved is off and flying with their own aspects of the unfolding vision. Believe me, your life will never be the same again after having spent even an hour in the true authority and connective presence of an evolutionary, visionary, transformative leader.

TRUE AUTHORITY
Authority, according to the dictionary, is 'the power or right to enforce obedience; delegated power; or person whose opinion is accepted, esp. expert in a subject.' But true authority is much more than any of this. True authority comes from tuning in to the potential of any moment and seeing from a far greater picture than self what's truly possible now. It's a greater understanding of what's occurring, why and where it can lead us.

People generally love to follow someone with true authority. With leaders working from and for a true authority, there's a strong sense of genuine trust, of rightness of purpose and of being led by and for something greater. But where does this true authority come from? Is it age and experience? Not really. Is it the wisdom of the ages

120

passed down to a very well trained few? No. True authority comes from connecting with something far greater than ourselves. It's about living in the knowing fields and working for Life in its fullest. True authority isn't that someone suddenly has THE TRUTH. In fact, there really are no truths … only a wide range of ever changing perspectives and potentials in every moment.

THE PLACE OF COLLECTIVE VISION

True authority speaks with a gentle yet passionate voice, excited by the possibilities on offer, calling others to be in their true authority too. New visionary leaders speak for our collective vision and are gifted their ability to lead because of the nature of their willingness to dive into something extraordinary, way beyond self.

The place of collective vision is a place where potential whispers at you from every corner, where the energy to make it real dances in your veins and where the tender, loving capacity to be someone you've always wanted to know rushes through you, transforming you from an ordinary human being into a new visionary leader. This is a place that everyone can access, that everyone can find their authority in and that everyone can shine through. True authority … it's about being a voice, a catalyst, an evolutionary agent for the greatest things imaginable now.

THE POWER OF CONNECTIVE PRESENCE

When I speak of presence, I'm not talking about personal presence … that's simply about your own capacity to shine using your personal energy. I'm talking about the power of connective presence that, like true authority, sources from this place of collective vision.

Connective presence is a powerful emanation of potentiality that reaches out to transform and aliven all those you connect with and everything you touch. New visionary leaders exude the power of this connective presence and know, as they do so, that it truly isn't about them. My good buddy Jane, who you'll read about in the next new visionary interview, used the word 'aeonic' one day and something about that called me to look into it further. When I looked up aeon in the dictionary, in addition to the definition around time (age of the universe; eternity), it also said 'A POWER EXISTING FROM ETERNITY.' Wow! How about that being in the dictionary? What if the power of connective presence is about emanating the true power of eternity, that even the dictionary acknowledges as real?

The power of connective presence is where new leadership for the 21st century really begins. It's here that we surrender into the magnificence of the moment to discover the alchemical art of being ... becoming transformative, alivening, creational catalysts for potentiality.

This new era requires nothing less of us than this. Standing at the doorway of the 21st century, we have huge goals in front of us ... the evolution of being, the creation of a vibrant new world and our conscious move into global and cosmic stewardship. To achieve these goals, we require a new kind of leadership that sources from a power source greater than ourselves. Now let me be clear ... I'm not pointing to our age old concepts of god, source, creator or anything like that, although I'm sure the argument could be made that it's all the same thing. I'm talking about the place of eternal Life source power, the place from whence our collective vision is born. This place, this energy, is simply sitting there waiting for us to tap into. It's ours to embrace, to embody, to exhilarate and to engage.

This is the power of connective presence. It's not about any one person's energy, beliefs, abilities, creativity or anything else. It's the power that comes from the source of our connectedness to everything. We're not just small human beings walking around trapped in individual bodies and minds. Truly we're not! We're vast, amazing, powerful beings of incredible capacity to source what's never been sourced before, to invent all things anew. It's here that we discover the magic of being who we really are in our fullest potential, not just as individuals, but as a race of beings passionately stirring the whirlwinds of evolution.

Let me introduce you to a magnificent example of this ... our thirteenth new visionary, my business partner and mega buddy, Jane MacAllister Dukes, a woman who brilliantly demonstrates the power of connective presence and the new authority that sources in knowing self and ALL.

NEW VISIONARY #13
JANE MACALLISTER DUKES
from the UK
Adventurer Extraordinaire!

I met Jane 6 years ago and my life hasn't been the same since. She's a wonderful new kind of rebel, an adventurer extraordinaire, an explorer of all things new and a creational being who's wrapping the world up in a huge embrace and zinging it into its fullest potential. She's my business partner and co-founder of The Evolutionary Network, as well as being one of the world's greatest mom's, a brilliant artist, a fabulous trainer and coach and more fun than you could imagine wrapped in one powerful woman's presence. Life would not be the same without her ... and I don't mean that just for me. I mean that for the whole of this world. It's my intention that this interview of a magnificent new visionary will inspire all those people out there who think that people who make a difference to the world have to be highly positioned leaders, well known authors or some such thing. For new visionaries, that's no longer true and Jane is a magnificent example of that. It's who she's being that's altering the world, every minute of every day. It oozes from her pores, streams out of her mouth and sparkles up everyone and everything she touches. I give you Jane MacAllister Dukes, adventurer extraordinaire.

A PURE DISPASSIONATE ADVENTURE

"The day I decided to drop everything and leap onto a square rigged sailing ship to circumnavigate the British Isles for 3 months, my mother gave me this quote from Robert Louis Stevenson: "All my life I have been after an adventure, a pure dispassionate adventure, such as befell early heroic voyagers" and that describes me to a 't.'

From the moment I could reflect, I was always puzzled by the way people did things. It never made sense. To me, they were upside down and backside foremost. I knew from a very early age that you could create whatever you wanted to. I came in as a creational being knowing that life wasn't like people said it was. I could never abide authority simply because I would not accept that what they said was so. I questioned most things I was taught and for this reason I was called a bit of a troublemaker or difficult. And yet I never understood why I should be considered difficult. I was just curious and asking what for me were obvious questions.

In my early life, I always felt like an observer, an outsider. I was never a part of things or belonged anywhere. It was curious to me that people were happy doing the same things all the time. I had many talents and capabilities and was continuously told that all I had to do was just choose one of them and concentrate on it and then I would succeed. But of course that was impossible for me. Try as I might, I couldn't do that.

I couldn't understand people's attachment to misery and pain. For me the world had infinitely more that was great and wonderful about it, than it had bad things. So it was natural for me to gravitate towards artists as they could really see and appreciate the beauty of things. I went to art school, though even there I didn't fit. It was only afterwards, when I started working in an avant-garde art gallery in Edinburgh, that I began to see that there were other people like me, but they were scattered all over the world.

I was lucky enough to know artists like Joseph Beuys, Gunther Uecker and Paul Neagu amongst others. Retrospectively I can see that these artists recognised who I was somehow. I understand that now and I'll never forget the support they gave me, which really helped to sustain me in what I thought was an upside down and insane world.

Because of all this, I've spent my life constantly seeking adventure, exploring and looking for what is and what isn't. When I started drawing again after many years enabling others in the gallery, the first drawings were absolutely about the physical and the metaphysical. Looking at my life, you could say that I lurched from one thing to another, but from my perspective that is absolutely not true. I was seeking and finding exactly the right experience and knowledge required for the work I'm really here to do ... the co-creation of a whole new world and beyond.

Now I am no longer alone and I've discovered that my early experience of being the outsider trained me magnificently to be sustainably consistent regarding any vision I might hold, no matter what anyone else around me might say. If it feels right and true to me, that's all I need to know.

This life long exploration brought me to the beginning of an understanding of energetics and consciousness. I began to realise that I had always worked this way. So when I met Soleira, it was almost a dream come true because not only did she also work with energy and consciousness, but she was intrigued by what I did and how I did it. This was illuminating to say the least because what she does is she deconstructs and reconstructs, thereby enabling explanations to occur around the architecting of this kind of work.

I came to realise through this process of co-analysis that everybody has these energetic abilities to see beyond what is. I see evidence for this everywhere I look. It's just that people are educated out of it at an early age and are taught these abilities aren't important or real, so they ignore or subvert them. If the abilities weren't subconscious in the first place, they would make them unconscious because of what other people thought or said about them, like 'that's just your imagination, that's not real, that's just a dream', etc. A good part of my work now is to awaken and empower others into the full realisation of who they really are so they too can use these wonderful innate abilities.

I bring who I am and the work I'm about to everything I do. This way of working in energetics and consciousness, which is me on legs, actually informs everything I do. I breathe it, sleep it, walk it, eat it, drink it and so on. It's not possible to be otherwise because I can't make myself separate from it all. I am a collective being.

We're all collective beings actually. That's another part of the work we're about in the world, to see that we are not separate, that 'no man is an island.'

Today, I know I have a conscious connectivity to many others that I didn't have before. But I'm under no illusion that I'm the same or that there's anyone else quite like me. I have a uniqueness that doesn't happen very often. In human terms that could be a difficult one to carry, but in cosmic terms it makes enormous sense.

OWNING AND LOVING ALL OF YOU

I think it's important for anyone who feels like that to recognise it and to be accepting of that. Because to work effectively you need to own and love all of you ... the most vulnerable parts of you, the most amazing parts of you, the darkest parts of you, the most powerful parts of you ... all of it. You have to love ALL of YOU. What starts to happen when you do that is that you can truly begin to be who you are. Up until that moment you're living a fragmented existence. For example, you may go off and meditate, play with your kids, be terrified about a job interview or have a washing disaster dyeing your husband's underpants pink. Having separate parts of you doing these different activities means you're fragmented. You need to bring all these parts of you together cosmiciously. You have to do all of these things in that beautiful state of grace of a totally connected, collective being. When you walk in life like that, magic begins to happen.

FALLING IN LOVE WITH LIFE

It's a bit like falling in love except that what you're doing is falling in love with Life itself. Falling in love with Life activates all your senses, so food starts to taste better, the sun shines brighter, you can smell the freshness of wild flowers. You're alive in a new way and you're no longer captivated by the man-made world.
I'm talking about more than just the man-made and the natural world. I might call it the phenomenology world. I read about phenomenologists when I was younger and I could see that they were touching on the unexplainable and the mystical, but trying to explain things in terms that weren't mystical. For me none of this is mystical. For me it's very, very real. Mystical means it's

126

strange, mysterious, unexplainable and unknowable and I can see how in human terms it can seem that way. But to me it's this other world that's real. I experience everything differently from an energetic place and I love living in a world of passion, possibility and potential. I've discovered that in fact I never did live in the normal 3D world. That's why I used to feel like an outsider. The normal 3D world was and is a needlessly restrictive framework. In the 3D world everything is conditional

THE FULLEST EXPRESSION OF EVERYONE EVERYWHERE
I could be called a rebel, but what am I rebelling against? I'm just being me and I always have been. I will not allow anyone ever again to reduce me in any way. It serves no one to allow that to occur. I stand for the fullest expression of everyone everywhere always ... their unique, magical, extraordinary and sadly, often self-limited, magnificence.

I'm making that so in the world by being unashamedly me at all times no matter what the circumstances. I love living in my full presence, as all that I am and as the collective possibilities that we are. That doesn't mean to say that I don't have respect for other people's beliefs, because of course I do. It's just that now other people's beliefs make no impression on me whatsoever. My experience tells me what's right and true. I know what I know and I live by that inner authority now. So I give these other beliefs no importance and therefore I can be with people in their belief systems in a more transformative way that doesn't offend them. You can allow things to alter graciously by being quiet and gently sure, sitting in a certainty of knowing in yourself without a need to convince or challenge anyone about it. Simply love them for their magnificence even beyond their beliefs. It's about being amazed and awed by their vastness and seeing them as big as you possibly can.

EVERY SINGLE BEING IS REMARKABLE
I walk in the knowing that every single being is remarkable. For example, a funny little uptight person in a black suit and high heels sitting in the corner is also a magnificent being. It's just that on some level that person is choosing not to be present right now.

127

Once I remind myself of this, then that's who I see them as and who I speak to. And it's amazing how gentle and transformative that conversation can be.

If this became a way of being for people, everything would change overnight. If we relate to people in this way and we're awake to who we truly are and all our amazing abilities, everything would alter massively and there would be no more wars and no more daft fights. Everything would be honoured, including the Earth for the wonderful being she is, and we would begin to understand the massive nature of creation and how staggering it is. Instead of all our smallness and fear, we'd be in hyper-creational mode, constantly discovering what new marvels we could come up with. If we could all just get access to the total passionate creational beings that we really are, on all the levels, then everybody would get their Godness back and Life would come alive in us all."

You Have Been Seen ... A poem by Jane MacAllister Dukes

You have been seen, it's no good now, hiding the truth of who you are
You have been seen we know the truth of who and what you really are
You are a vast amazing being with gifts beyond your wildest dreams
Vibrant, new imaginings are bursting at your seams

The source of you is infinite, well beyond a human measure
Beyond all thoughts that you may have, or any human pleasure
The vibrant, wondrous source of you can't wait for you to realise
Just what you can co-create, unfolding soon before your eyes

Come on it says, come dance with me, breathe, relax, expand
Engage with me, the source of you, come on and take my hand
The source of you is magic, it resides in every cell
Your knowing tells you this is true and now it wants to yell

Wake up, don't hide, come on rejoice, the time is now and here
Listen to your own source voice and then let out a cheer
When you step up and really own, the alchemy of all of you
At last you'll be the one you know, a leader, tall and true

THE ART OF EXCELLENCE

There's just one last thing that I want to touch on for this book and that's the art of excellence. All of the great ones ... artists of every kind ... know the art of excellence. Without it, books are just words, art is just brush strokes and speaking is just sound.

The art of excellence isn't just about being finicky or a perfectionist. It's about reaching into this well spring of potentiality, into Life's sourceful energy, and calling GREATNESS through you. It's not about greatness for yourself, although that's often a fallout of it. It's greatness for its own accord. The art of excellence has us reach beyond ourselves to find that which will stir Life, call forth the best in all of us and create a wave of motion that alivens the world and beyond!

Excellence is a fire from which we draw our passions. It's an opportunity to touch the eternal in us all. Stars, galaxies and gases paint pictures for us across the cosmicious skies. We have the same ability to create an eternal combustion of brilliant, breathtaking splendour. When we put pen to paper or brush to canvas, or even if we're cleaning up the kitchen sink, we can touch the stars in everything, calling the next kaleidoscopic swirl into creation.

As you can see, I'm just talking about artists. I'm talking about people and the new leadership that stirs within them. Leaders who can touch the cosmic swirls of potentiality, who dance in the infinite symphony of the spheres, who carry with them the brilliance that every one of us can be, passing it on to every other being they touch. This is the new leadership of the 21st century. You can forget about the old ways now. You can step into the genuine knowing, the true authority, the sourceful power and the connective presence of a leader who leads through a commitment to the art of excellence, to a life that stretches far beyond self.

Do you feel that place inside you where you know without a shadow of a doubt that we are MORE? The place where greatness reaches out its hand to you? The place where all things are possible and you are the source of making them so?

To excel is to live a life of passionate leaps towards greatness for us all. You can live as this, in every moment ... not just when you're up front leading or creating something artistic. The art of excellence is a state of being that's sourced from that wondrous, infinite place where our collective vision resides. And that means that it's yours, mine and ours always and with it we can write a new script for ourselves as vast beings of enormous capacity.

What will you choose now that you know that so much more is on offer to you? How will you lead from here? Can you go back for even one second and live as less than you really are? I believe that this book, this writing, this vision that is ours on the biggest evolutionary scales, will call you into something brilliantly brand new. And the great news is that as you step into the excellence of your new leadership, whatever that looks like for you, then many others will go with you into that new place along with you. It's inherent in our connective design now. As one takes the leap, all others resonantly connected with that person, take the leap as well. So big breath ... and take the big leap into the art of visionary'ism and excellence. Don't hold back and don't think small. You're the possibility of something magnificently brand new for us all.

NEW VISIONARY #14
SOLEIRA GREEN
Taking on the World

"Having said all else, I guess that brings it round to me, Soleira Green, global visionary. I want to use my story to inspire every single person out there to stand up and take on big, bigger and the very biggest things they can possibly imagine. Why? Because it will give you the most magnificent, magical, awe-inspiring life!

I certainly didn't start life as a global visionary. I started life as a simple, small town, Canadian girl. Yup, just like everybody else, I grew up normal, hardly even knowing the rest of the world existed. We just barely had television sets back then and the world seemed an awfully BIG place. I didn't have any of these amazing abilities and I certainly had no idea the world of energy even existed. I was passionately interested in things beyond the norm, but probably no more than most people with an intelligent, seeking mind.

I remember there was a time in my adult life, well after my first marriage had broken up and my second longer term relationship had ended in disaster, that someone said to me that I had so many walls around me, that she couldn't sit in a car with me. My energy was pressing her out the window. I was aghast. I had no idea anyone could tell I was walled off and suffering inside. This insight marked the beginning of a very wonderful awakening.

It was at a transformative moment at my dad's funeral in 1984 that I finally decided not to waste another precious moment of life on things that didn't count for anything ... the big job, the huge aspirations, the organisational politics and working my self to the bone for a company that didn't seem to notice.

So I began my journey of transformation and I have loooooved every single minute of it. If I died tomorrow, I can truly say that I have LIVED and LOVED and that I have made more difference to people and to this world than I could have imagined was EVER possible.

It was in 1996, in a moment of connecting with something far greater than myself, that I kept hearing a prodding voice (very likely my own on some level of me) cajoling and urging me to step up to the proverbial plate and take on the world. 'What!', I exclaimed, 'You must be kidding. I'm just a small town Canadian girl. I can't change the world.' But the voice continued and the urgings flowed on until I knew I had to surrender. Something far bigger than me was going on here. So I stood up and said 'YES, I'll do it.'

From that moment on, Life has constantly surprised me. I've been given everything I need to make this happen. I live in a different world. Words pour out of my fingertips as I write and out of my mouth when I'm called to speak. Energy vibrates through me with euphoric abandon. I fall in love with so many people a month that it's hard to keep count. I have the best friends in the whole world and we're doing the most amazing work together. I have an incredible husband who shares this groundbreaking work with me and is an extraordinary leader in his own right. I'm exhilarated by my work, which is never separate from my Life. I live this 24/7 and it's more passionate, exciting and adventuresome than I could have ever imagined. I travel the world, meeting amazing people, visiting incredible places and revelling in the gorgeousness of Life here on planet Earth.

I've sourced a body of work that provides source solutions for all that we trouble over in this world. The energetic and consciousness world has always held the key to it all. It only took me becoming an energy sensitive ten years ago to discover just who it was that really knew what would turn the world around. All those energetically aware people had always had the answer. They just were being overwhelmed by everyone else's view of the world. The answer lies in our ability to connect ... with ourselves, with one another and with everything. And so I began the co-creational journey of evolving vibrant energetics, conscious living, transformative being and connective consciousness with all these amazing, energetically aware people.

You can see by reading this book what wonderful insights, discoveries and abilities have come to the fore from it all. I don't need to recap it here. But I do want to say one thing and I want you to realise that this is being said by a 5 ft. 2 in. tall woman who comes from regular old stock in a small town in the middle of nowhere.

Before I leave this planet, in this lifetime, there will be no more wars, no more hunger, abundance will be available to all and people will be seen, honoured and recognised for the extraordinarily magnificent beings that they really are. I'm not taking this on as if taking the problematic world on my shoulders. I'm taking it on from the source of the vibrant, joyful, delicious potential that we, the Earth and the cosmos really are. I am / we are at work on the source solutions to all these things and they are already shifting faster than anyone could have possibly imagined. I'm not saying it egotistically, but I am saying it boldly, transformatively and with all the true power of my full being. You can count on me for this.

You see, we are all extraordinary beings who can no longer hide behind the mask of ordinary human being. We are out of the closet and at work, individually and collectively, to do what it is we're here to do. I'm here to say that for me there is no greater life than this. So if you've finished reading this book and you're pondering what to do around your own new visionary leadership, I urge you to dive in with great abandon and know that the water is not only fine, but that we are surfing the unridden, newly created realm magnificently.

You see I'm no longer Soleira Green, human being, doing some good things for the Earth. I'm a collective being of vast intelligence, incredible strength and alivening energy who is, along with every one of you, transforming this planet and beyond! When we complete with this life, we will look back in awe and wonder at that which we have done here. We are doing the impossible, shifting aeons of possibility into a new world now and that will ripple through the cosmoses and alter consciousnesses and Life everywhere. I am moved to tears constantly by the beauty of who we are and the brilliance of what we're doing together here. This is it! And I want to say that it just doesn't get any better than that!

As I complete this book, I wish you great fun, lots of abundance, amazing friends on the journey and fulfilling evolutionary work throughout the whole of your life. For myself I know that on the day that I complete life on Earth, I will look back to these moments of myself as an evolutionary visionary and say 'Wow, that was FANTASTIC! Bring on the next biggest game.' May your life be completely fulfilling for you in all that you do and may we dance together in the celebration of our greatest creation … a splendiferous new world."